SMOKE AND MIRRORS: STRATEGIC SELF-AWARENESS FOR LEADERS AND FUTURE LEADERS

SMOKE AND MIRRORS: STRATEGIC SELF-AWARENESS FOR LEADERS AND FUTURE LEADERS

Learn How to Tackle Denials and Blind Spots and Achieve Political Awareness and Alignment

ELIZABETH DULBERGER

ISBN-13: 9781546328858
ISBN-10: 1546328858

I dedicate this book to my son, Preston,
a charismatic, creative, tough, and morally sound future leader.

ACKNOWLEDGMENTS

I would like to express my gratitude to many people who saw me through this book project: to all who provided support, allowed me to interview them, answered questions, offered comments, allowed me to quote their remarks and expressed their stories, and assisted in editing and proofreading and in the overall design of this book.

Thank you to all my clients and friends who dedicated much of their valuable time communicating their perspectives, giving me ideas, telling their stories, reading and rereading full chapters, and encouraging me in this process. The wealth of my knowledge and success comes from my incredibly talented and compassionate clients who allowed me to see into their thought processes, organizational structures, and decision making.

I would like to thank my family, who lovingly supported me throughout this book project. With two beautiful little kids, client responsibilities, speaking engagements, and a busy travel schedule, I could have never done this without their help: my husband, Guy; my mom, Alina; my dad, Sam; my brother, Boris; and my mother- and father-in-law, Anca and Marian. A very heartfelt thank-you to my dear friend, and ultimate voice of reason Tom Schwartz, without whom I wouldn't be who I am today.

I would also like to thank Sunamita Lim, my dedicated and patient editor; thank you for your continuous encouragement to speak my truth.

Finally, I thank my strong, powerful, and generous grandmother Olga, who recently passed away. She continues to be my secret weapon—my strength, resilience, and perseverance.

My apologies to those who supported me over the years and are unintentionally not mentioned here.

FOREWORD

I was thrilled to learn that Liz is writing a book and was deeply honored when she asked me to write this foreword. Her willingness to put her ideas onto these pages and share them with the world is a testament to her character and her passion for connecting with people from all walks of life. I have seen these traits in her over our long friendship, which has been filled with mutual mentorship, deep understanding, and shared growth. From the day we met, Liz was always deeply interested in my time in public office, as well as my service in the US Army. These passions for politics and public service demonstrate her zeal to fight for those she serves.

Despite her passion for politics, Liz has never served in public office. Yet she has a rare innate talent to connect with everybody, regardless of their age, title, or socioeconomic status. I have always been amazed by her ability to relate to—and counsel—high-powered executives and then moments later have an authentic connection with ordinary individuals. This is a skill I see in seasoned politicians, but not often do I see it in someone so young. This unusual gift has allowed Liz to gain the trust of entry-level young professionals to C-suite executives. If they have been able to benefit from her advice, I believe you will too.

As you delve into the pages that follow, you will embark on a journey filled with exceptionally thought-provoking stories and ideas. Regardless of where you are in your career, I am confident that you will profit from this clever, poignant, and incredibly honest first book.

Enjoy the adventure.

Valde Garcia

Valde Garcia

Retired State Senator, Retired US Army Officer

CONTENTS

INTRODUCTION

The supreme quality for leadership is unquestionably integrity. Without it, no real success is possible, no matter whether it is on a section gang, a football field, in an army, or in an office.

—Dwight D. Eisenhower

Throughout this book, you will see four main concepts repeated: self-awareness, alignment, mutual benefit, and integrity. These four concepts, together with a strong sense of political awareness, are the pillars for success that rising stars and established high-level leaders need to be acutely aware of.

Truly allowing yourself opportunities to dig deep and understand why they are so vital to achieving all your goals and continuing to apply them in all areas of life is crucial.

May this book help you become more aware of how unique, capable, deserving, and resourceful you are.

I want to encourage you to continue serving humanity the best way you know how, to continuously help those around you grow, develop, and manifest your and their desired futures.

Elizabeth Dulberger

PART 1
GUTS AND GLORIES

Chapter 1

● ● ●

WHY ALIGNING WITH GOOD LEADERS MATTERS

*Leadership and learning are
indispensable to each other.*

—JOHN FITZGERALD KENNEDY

Most of us want to rise *fast*, and once we do, we want to make sure we are influential and make a difference (or you wouldn't be reading my book). I'm also driven to succeed, to stay successful—and to continue helping others succeed as a leadership coach. There are two key ingredients empowering our professional sprint to the top—and staying there as influential leaders.

These ingredients are (a) self-awareness, and (b) alignment with other influencers, such as bosses and powerful people, plus their ideas and projects.

"Fast risers" have the capacity to develop authentic self-awareness and the empowered belief in the self that continuously propels them to want to learn, get knocked down, learn from mistakes, and emerge even stronger.

A simple roadmap for cultivating leadership success is made up of five elements:

1. Show up with a strong presence.
2. Figure out what's going on *fast*.
3. Locate key players.
4. Create a plan to problem-solve a pressing issue using every resource at your disposal.
5. Spend quality time influencing people to work with you.

Natural leaders are action driven and improvement driven. This is an instinctive trait; they can't help it. Leaders gravitate toward moving forward and are determined in making progress. If you're lucky enough to work beside them or under them, you'll make boundless progress too.

QUALITIES OF FAST RISERS

- Your desire to take on risks, with the goal of producing *credible* results.

- Speaking your mind, even if it's unpopular at the moment (however, many fear this and prefer to coast).

- If on a team, you're driven to succeed in every project the team is given.

- Your willingness to become the face of the department, project, or idea.

- Holding yourself 100 percent accountable at all times (and not blaming others).

- Understanding that likability isn't just about charm, that it includes holding people accountable and commanding respect from them.

ALIGN WITH A FOCUSED LEADER

One of my clients, a senior vice president (SVP) of finance at a large firm, was first hired as a director with two people reporting to her, her trusted right hands. She appreciated their support in her new role; both of them *just knew* they were working for a real leader. In a very brief period, she helped advance them to where both now hold positions equal to hers.

These two right hands saw in my client the desire to drive forward and mentor her staff. They supported her with unwavering loyalty; they were eager to learn. She rewarded them with opportunities to develop their professional progress and to learn along with her. Over time, the improvements she made at this company were significant. She worked well with her team identifying problem issues and created projects to improve upon these issues. Both learned from her natural leadership ability and stood by her to deliver exceptional progress. Little did they know they had become synonymous and aligned with my client when senior leaders spoke of this SVP, plus her projects and successes.

MOVING FORWARD FAST WITH A GOOD LEADER

In this book, I will often refer to developing relationships and partnering with strong and authentically confident key people. It is important to understand where the power plays are. To know how these power plays shift continuously so *you* benefit from aligning with good leaders—who in turn can help you rise more quickly.

I met James when he was a junior marketing manager who worked for the vice president (VP) of sales and marketing for the past six months. However, after this short period, he started developing a trusted professional relationship with the company CEO. How did James do it?

As most CEOs are, this CEO was concerned about having new, positive company initiatives to discuss with the board. His strategy was to continuously generate support from his board and demonstrate that their company was operating very well, particularly by highlighting initiatives they carried out compared to competition. It was important to the CEO that his management team was continuously focused on initiatives that made this company stand out from others.

Initially, James didn't know about the CEO's strategy, as he was a relatively junior member of the team. However, because he was a natural quick riser, he identified key players early on, identified his boss's motive, and anticipated a problem he could solve. He noticed his boss's enthusiasm when she came to their team meetings to generate singular ideas for the CEO. James and I had been working together for two months when he brought this up during our weekly calls. My antenna immediately shot up. "This is his opportunity!" This young leader inspires me with how observant he is, how keenly aware he is. I knew I had a natural leader on my hands; with the slightest push in the right direction, he would soar even higher.

If James helped his VP generate great ideas for the CEO, the CEO would reward the VP. In turn, he would be rewarded. If this happened continuously, James would have a spotlight on himself in no time and become the face of the team. My mind was running away with every possibility I envisioned for James's success. I knew he saw them, too. *James must ride the opportunity and momentum wave now—not lose a moment.*

James needed to develop a great marketing initiative to beat other companies in their industry and to present it at the meeting with a list of "requirements, problems, project time, and issues that may arise." After a week of vigorously researching marketing initiatives at other companies (outside of their industry), calling friends and past colleagues, connecting with a few marketing folks on LinkedIn, and messaging previous marketing bosses, James came up with an initiative he thought the VP would love to take back to the CEO as a "bragging opportunity." He knew that if he succeeded, it would accomplish two things:

1. Shine a light on his department for the CEO.
2. Shine the first of many lights on him as an up and coming face of the department, one the VP can rely on to deliver innovative and practical results.

James's initiative gave the VP a brand-new perspective on how James thought and operated. The VP was astonished he understood what lay behind her requests, and that he understood her desire to deliver unique ideas to the CEO. In turn, James was rewarded with her ear and support.

HOW TO ALIGN WITH FORWARD-MOVING LEADERS

Think like them, in alignment with their professional-personal and company values:

- ✓ Embrace loyalty (to project leader *and* the company's overall success).
- ✓ Study the environment, identify issues, and create solutions.
- ✓ Fill in gaps on the leader's behalf; watch his or her blind spot.
- ✓ Develop resilience and self-esteem to stay confident through the inevitable lows.
- ✓ Be accountable, direct, and transparent when working with leaders.

SPONSORSHIP

Rising stars need to also learn that they must spend time with powerful sponsors who are not only mentors. Sylvia Ann Hewlett in her book *Forget a Mentor, Get a Sponsor* (2013) advised risers to surround themselves with influencers who are ready to invest their names and perhaps even money behind them. Sponsors are different from mentors. Mentors advise and bring you lessons they've acquired over the course of their lives and careers. However, as great as that is, they have nothing on the line when it comes to helping you; but sponsors do.

WHAT IT MEANS TO HAVE A SPONSOR

- ✓ When someone powerful and influential puts his or her reputation on the line for you (or their money through an investment in you), this is true sponsorship.
- ✓ When an influencer has something to gain from helping you (in being recognized as the person who recognized your talents).
- ✓ To deserve this sponsorship, you need to possess the skill sets, talent, and unremitting drive to excel so as not to let down this sponsor.
- ✓ Your work *must* be exceptional behind his or her endorsement; or people will question what you did to get the endorsement.

✓ The relationship should evolve naturally and organically and be mutually beneficial.

✓ When you have a sponsor, you cannot rely only on him or her for your success. You must blaze and hustle forward like you still don't have it all—and to use your sponsorship only as a "cherry or the topping" to validate your hard work.

✓ When you have opened some doors, relying heavily on your sponsorship without showing your talent will have your sponsor reconsidering his or her original decision.

HOW TO KNOW WHEN YOU'VE FOUND YOUR SPONSOR

Paradoxically, sponsors will highlight and support some of the qualities other colleagues and executives may have previously criticized you on. Perhaps sponsors are above being threatened, insecure, or self-serving because they're eminently successful in what they do. Whatever the reasons, it pays to develop an instinct to know who would be a good-match sponsor for you. Dig deep. You will discover who this could be or you will discover that it's time for you to use every resource at your disposal to get out there and impress your future sponsor.

LIZ'S TIPS FOR ALIGNING WITH GOOD LEADERS

- True inner confidence, a backbone, and conviction are three key qualities to look for in a great leader.

- Your new boss will hire you for what you can do. Your current boss will value you for what you have already done. The best boss is the current one who values you for what you can still do.

- Those closest to you may value your stock lower than those who don't yet know you. When presenting yourself to new people and situations, aim higher.

- The more invested someone is in your future, the more you will benefit. Spend time attracting those who can take credit for your eventual success.

- Suit up with resilience to take on the challenges that you will inevitably face on the way up. Align with the right influencers to make your ride to the top less bumpy.

Chapter 2

● ● ●

HONING YOUR LEADERSHIP AND ENTREPRENEURIAL EDGE

*It's fine to celebrate success but it's more
important to heed the lessons of failure.*

—BILL GATES

L et me emphasize this all-important point: advancing at an early
age has everything to do with raw abilities and intelligence. You
need to be extremely self-aware. Know if you can meet challenges
head on. Meaning, you *are* emotionally and professionally mature
beyond your chronological years. Clearly, if you don't believe in
yourself, neither will anyone else.

The three essential tools you must have in your *Foundation Toolkit* are as follows:

1. *Raw entrepreneurial ability* in *just* feeling what and how to "do it"
2. *Influential resources and sponsors* to support you with credible, expert advice
3. *Inner strength and perseverance* to battle through challenges, never giving up

THE FOUNDATION TOOLKIT: BUILDING ON SOLID GROUND
1. RAW ABILITY

I cannot stress enough on having the raw ability to power through as a leader. You need to know you're able to work at the level you're trying to reach. You need complete self-assurance in your capabilities as a leader. Your confidence cannot be shaky, not outwardly anyway. You need to believe in your raw intelligence and resourcefulness; you need to be capable, and you need to believe very authentically in your capabilities.

If you do not completely feel all this today, don't panic. This doesn't mean you will not reach this level of belief in yourself. You will know when that feeling uncovers itself deep down—past doubts, insecurities, and especially other people's opinions will slowly drift away. Until then, keep looking deep and discovering how smart and capable you are. Unfortunately, illusions and denials will not carry you through to the top; these don't work long term, and if they do, it comes at a very high price for the soul.

You need a solid foundation before you start your business or begin climbing that corporate ladder—and make sure it is sitting on solid ground. This solid ground mainly consists of a strong belief in oneself. Otherwise, cracks in the ground will start forming. These cracks are mainly developed by other people's agendas; the ladder can get quite heavy once you start climbing. When cracks form, it means the ground wasn't solid enough when you started your journey. At this point, go back and realize your incredible potential, renew your belief in yourself, gather even more sponsors and resources—and start again.

Raw ability and raw determination are felt strongly inside, but external factors and the pursuit of greater knowledge are also components of raw ability. These include

(a) a wide range of education;

(b) in-depth knowledge of yourself including your weaknesses;

(c) continuous curiosity and lifelong learning; and

(d) a wide network of resources of people (outside the company you work for) who can help when you face challenges.

2. RESOURCES

I am a big fan of utilizing every resource at your disposal. I am cautious around people who won't ask for help or admit that others can be and have been helpful to them. Surround yourself with qualified, intelligent, and skilled people to turn to for advice. Here I am, an executive coach; yet I continuously need help and expert resources to equip me with greater knowledge when assisting my clients. This strategy gives me access to great minds to turn to for clarification and a range of in-depth analyses. We have professionals for a reason. Many individuals have spent decades perfecting their craft, all the better to help and guide you. My clients guide me all the time. I am lucky to be surrounded with incredibly accomplished and successful individuals I turn to for help. I don't pretend I know it all.

New leaders are most vulnerable and absolutely must surround themselves with resources. You cannot do it all alone. Even though every fiber of your being wants to believe it's you against the world, the truth is, it's much easier with key people on your side, showing you how to navigate your uphill climb. Take for instance this story.

A client was offered a VP of Development position at age thirty-four. He was uncertain about this offer, even though he was a talented software engineer and programmer. However, since I knew him well, I felt he was ready to take this on. He said there were areas of complex coding he didn't yet understand. The chief technology officer (CTO) who offered him this role expected projects to get off the ground ASAP. My client was to lead a team of six programmers who also didn't have the high-level technical knowledge required.

I advised him to say, "Yes, absolutely! What an honor! Thank you!" My strategy was to get busy figuring out how he can deliver those required competencies. In one of our phone sessions, I asked if he could just Google for those codes; he laughed, but it moved us closer to an idea.

"There must be a way," I pushed.

"Who can you ask for help?"

"Can you personally pay a young brilliant programmer while he stays on the phone with you to explain the ropes?" He laughed at all my ideas.

A few days later, he called to say all this talk about getting help was having an effect. It made him realize two things:

1. He could not ruin this amazing opportunity to professionally advance in his career.

2. How little his world was, with limited resources and a limited network.

His self-awareness hit him hard. He knew he needed expert resources for advice; his whole team would be looking up to him. Over the weekend, he reached out to two CTOs and two senior software engineers in different states, in completely different industries. He found them on LinkedIn, the business-networking site.

He asked if they'd be interested in a mentorship relationship; in turn, he offered to mentor someone junior on their teams and to be available as a resource for any support they might need to deliver on their projects in his area of expertise. He didn't get a reply. When he told me this, I saw leadership qualities in him that made me realize his self-awareness (particularly his weaknesses) were taking him to new heights of progress. He identified his weaknesses, he accepted that he may not have what it takes at the moment, and instead of closing the door to this opportunity, he decided to reach out for support, to barter. He was protecting himself, and empowering himself with people who can help him succeed.

The lesson here? The only way this route will work is if you believe deep down that you will quickly catch up to the requirements of the role. To start cultivating confidence and skill levels needed for the job, or the opportunity would crash and burn.

A few weeks later, after sending out more e-mails, he heard from a software engineer of a small Seattle tech company. They went back and forth about their specialties and figured they could support each other with whatever the other needed.

MUTUAL BENEFIT

Tom, the software engineer in Seattle, was unsure about his future at his tech start-up, as it depended upon the company's funding, success, and survival. I believe Tom felt in my client a sense of stability (a young, accomplished leader who accepted a job with a stable company). In case Tom's new venture didn't work out, he saw possibilities with this new connection (my client). In turn, my client had access to a brilliant coding mind which helped him understand new levels of coding. As I emphasize often, mutually beneficial relationships work. Their relationship flourished.

As my client progressed with his new position, his mentoring relationship allowed him access to a like-minded, intelligent individual who helped him reach new coding levels (of course this wasn't without a ton of reading and research he had to do outside of this mentoring). A few months into his job, I helped him put together a proposal to hire a junior programmer, who possessed coding requirements for this role so my client could focus and elevate his attention on the department's strategic direction and development. This move, together with all his recently acquired knowledge, covered his bases as well as the company. Tom could only take my client so far—but it gave him the confidence to persevere, as he continued forming new relationships similar to this initial one.

> **As an executive coach, I see how underestimated interrelated networking relationships are. When clients are flying toward promotions and recognition, they forget how important networking available resources are, to help leverage their advancement opportunities.**

OTHERS ARE READY TO HELP

When I first entered a brand-new industry at a young age, I realized very quickly I could not succeed without resources. I came off my delusional high horse, knelt on the ground, surrounded myself with industry experts and senior leaders, and humbly asked their help. Most people don't realize how willing others are to help. People build upon their self-confidence and self-worth when they assist others; many are very willing to do it. Most young, ambitious people don't realize how much quicker they could climb with networking resources.

More experienced people are not on the opposite side. They're often very willing to come alongside to help you succeed. Truth be told, many are honored you asked and once they have put their energies into helping you, they usually don't stop as they now feel invested.

I'm happy to report that my once shy, incredibly resourceful client now works in Seattle; this relationship did more for him than what he'd initially intended. Once the founders of the start-up met him, they had to have him. Once again, he said, "Yes! I'm honored; thank you!" and then called me to ask, "Can I really do this? This is taking a huge risk; it could fail. What about moving on, with the stability of a paycheck?"

The point of this story is, you never know what your networking resources can do for you. One opportunity often leads to another in this fascinating life. Exposing your vulnerabilities to others and asking for their assistance is a quality of strength, not weakness. In this situation, my client ended up with a rewarding, challenging entrepreneurial executive role, and a friend. I ended up with new clients in Seattle, and a successful team I'm honored to work with to this day. Be prepared to ride the momentum when you see the opportunity coming your way.

3. INNER STRENGTH AND PERSEVERANCE

You must be emotionally strong and resilient to handle all kinds of punches coming at you. Some of these punches will not be overtly displayed or even remotely noticed on the surface, such as well-meaning advice from loved ones and coworkers. People will try to shake the ladder, or cut out some steps; some will want you to fall off for various self-serving reasons. Outdated social norms expect a lot of hard work and many years to rise to the top—I call this the "gray-hair confidence." I feel this is a very shortsighted attitude. Whatever it takes, you need to be ready for surprising punches, even if it means wearing a gray wig to throw some folks off.

FOUR TIPS FOR HONING YOUR LEADERSHIP EDGE

Here are four vital tips for honing your leadership edge:

1. Solve problems again and again (privately and publicly).
2. Learn from accomplished leaders.

3. Give them what they need, and they will give you what you want.

4. Keep your soul clean.

1. BECOME THE PROBLEM-SOLVER

Find out the place that almost everyone in the company is trying to avoid. You need to take it head on. This is the place for a person who has to figure out solutions to problems, people concerns, team concerns, project deadlines, etc. Look around. Those hiding from being appointed seldom reach leadership roles. You don't need to be in a titled position to take on such responsibilities, truly a tough challenge. Win or lose, you're in the spotlight, and a risky position to be in. However, in my opinion, without taking it on, you're not getting anywhere.

One way to be seen as the problem-solver is to make suggestions to your boss or in meetings. When the boss finds it a great idea, volunteer to lead, and get the team ready to implement (even if there are more senior people on the same team). The key lies in the way you make that offer. It must be nonthreatening, to come from a position of trying to help the team succeed. Think: "I will sacrifice if it helps my hard-working boss get this project in on time." Make these offers with an audience and sometimes just to your boss alone, giving him or her an opportunity to give you responsibility without setting off red flags to the rest of the team. When senior staff is faced with a large team of people many of whom deserve promotions based on seniority, bosses will be very careful who gets singled out in front of their teams. In private though, out of the desire to succeed, they will always appoint the more competent, enthusiastic, and diligent one. So, move into this role!

> **The key, as with everything, is balancing the number of times you solve problems publicly versus privately for the person who can promote you. You need to become the "secret right hand," the public supporter, and "taking one for the team" in adroitly managing all at the same time.**

If you do this successfully, you can count on quick advancements. Those around you will no longer question your age or competence. You've set yourself up as the "go-to." Your ability to bag opportunities of course goes back to your raw ability to deliver on tasks, persevere when things don't go your way, and tapping resources/people/sponsors who can guide you through.

One client pulled this off naturally and magically. I was shocked to see how quickly he jumped at opportunities, at age twenty-six. However, he wasn't aware of the need to be armed with a foundation toolkit for taking on big opportunities. He took responsibility for larger projects he didn't have skill sets for. However, when you're on fire and extremely motivated, you rarely listen to advice—even when you're paying for it.

It took me weeks to convince him to add to his foundation toolkit. I asked him every week if he'd be interested in a project-management course. His adrenalin though kept telling him he could accomplish anything (of which I'm a huge fan—*but* only when the foundation toolkit has been opened, reflected on, and mastered).

After weeks, I finally convinced him to start a project-management course he personally paid for in March 2015. Come August 2015 he took on a team project-leader role. He secretly shared with his boss that he was studying hard to be more useful to her. He didn't tell his team that he used every advanced project-management tool he learned to bring their project to a successful completion. He even had a visit from the vice president thanking him in getting on with their programs, and for the swift completion.

These two points are also critical:

i. Cross-department exposure (volunteering to take charge at any level for positive exposure).

ii. Balancing your act. You can't be too fearful of taking on responsibilities because you feel you don't have the foundation skills; at the same time, you cannot recklessly take on initiatives without reflecting on what needs augmenting or enhancing in the foundation toolkit.

2. LEARN FROM ACCOMPLISHED LEADERS

It's amazing how far you can go when you're genuinely interested and impressed with the accomplishments of leaders. When you express a real interest in how they got to where they are now, and skills needed to advance, you're creating an ally. I still hear from a previous boss (when I was twenty-four) and new to the corporate world. He said to me, "I've not had another employee who was as interested in my business as you were."

I was genuinely curious about how this man built his empire. I was an assistant back then. I stayed very close to powerful leaders. He taught me a lot; simply because I asked questions that took him down memory lane and gave him opportunities to reflect on what he had built, which was a quick boost to self-worth for him.

Every week I asked for a different story. He told me how he landed his first client. It impressed me no end. He was unprepared to deliver on his promises but had a network of people who wanted to help him succeed. He pulled through and built a large business. I instinctively knew I wouldn't often be around a person who had created such successful projects. I wanted to soak it all up. Every chance I could, I asked about a different accomplishment, and wrote down all the "struggles" he had to overcome. I still have that journal today and often refer to it for inspiration when my entrepreneurial clients are going through their struggles.

I cannot stress how genuine this curiosity has to be; you need to truly want to learn from accomplished people. You cannot fake this interest, if you do it will eventually fade and the executive will know you were just brown-nosing. This curiosity will truly make them feel accomplished. They have all overcome struggles; seen rejection, competition, termination, jealousies, shrewd bosses, exhibited loyalties; and discovered their passions through hardships.

Accomplished pros are here to teach you. Take a *genuine* interest in their journeys. You'll be amazed what they'll do for your career. They'll reward you for giving them an opportunity to teach you and speak about their journey because nobody asks them and more importantly not many appreciate their stories if they do get asked. All it took was a genuine willingness to learn from this accomplished, generous, respected man—and I acquired a lifelong sponsor.

3. GIVE THEM WHAT THEY NEED; THEY'LL GIVE YOU WHAT YOU WANT

This is simple; give whatever these leaders need from you to allow them to shine. However, be aware of red flags to look for in bosses and spot dead ends (see chapter 6). When you've decided that this person is a good-fit leader who will encourage and inspire you, the one who wants you to succeed, then by all means, *help them succeed* by giving them what they need. No task is too small or beneath you, no project is too much for you. Figure it out and make them look good.

Some of my clients challenge me on this idea. They say if they become indispensable their boss will never present them with opportunities from having it too good. I disagree. The best leader leaves a trail of leaders behind them (not one leader, but a trail). Just as they encourage you to go on achieving your successes, they'll attract other motivated, smart persons to lead whom they will eventually liberate, too. It has happened to me and to my clients; we gave our all in working for the right, forward-looking leader and we were released towards greater opportunities.

4. KEEP YOUR SOUL CLEAN; SHOW INTEGRITY

On your way up, avoid taking unfortunate actions; their consequences could derail everything you've built. I cannot stress integrity enough. Don't do "whatever it takes to succeed." Draw a morality boundary for your soul, and don't cross it for anyone. You *will* be seduced and tested as you climb. Reach into your foundation toolkit for inner strength. Find the strength to turn away from deception, corruption, throwing people under the bus, or losing your compassion.

> **As you speed toward success, be sure not to run over anyone while speeding over the bumps. There will come a time when you'll have to go back to that spot, see the bodies, acknowledge your actions, and face those consequences.**

HONING YOUR ENTREPRENEURIAL EDGE

What does it take to become an entrepreneur? Four important qualities are important for honing your entrepreneurial capabilities:

1. Entrepreneurship must run in your blood.
2. You are constantly sharpening your common sense and good judgment.
3. You are like a chameleon, in learning and absorbing business smarts.

4. You are acutely aware of the need to be in alignment—with your business goals and operations, and evolving partnerships you form.

1. ENTREPRENEURSHIP MUST RUN IN YOUR BLOOD

This doesn't mean entrepreneurship cannot be learned, but only through an intensely strong passion that exists innately. When your heart and guts speak loudly, listen. Even those who say they were not born entrepreneurs admit some decisions "just came" to them naturally and they knew the answers, had the judgment, and had the urgency to rise to the occasion in working through issues.

Be very careful if you are choosing this path *based on any of the following as the sole and strongest reason to peruse entrepreneurship*:

- ✓ You despise and cannot work with authority figures.
- ✓ You were terminated, or quit, and cannot place yourself.
- ✓ It's the trendy thing to do at the moment.
- ✓ You have family money to fall back on or to people willing to help you if you're struggling.
- ✓ You feel you're limited in the amount of money you can make as an employee.

✓ As a professional (accountant, lawyer, etc.) you get seduced as you watch your entrepreneurial clients make money by running their own businesses; and you want to do the same (see the story below).

2. YOU MUST DEVELOP COMMON SENSE AND GOOD JUDGMENT

Studies show most successful business people consider common sense as the foundation for their success. Common sense is the ability to make sound judgments in daily situations you encounter.

Common sense allows you to understand complex issues in simpler terms, to get to the core of a problem, solve it quickly, and to keep running forward with workable solutions.

When I get asked how I made a particular decision or had a perspective on how things could turn out for a client, my answer usually is "common sense." However, I have learned over the years that common sense is not that common. When you become an entrepreneur without a full company backing up your ideas, it gets very tough. You're no longer Mr. Bob Smith, VP of impressive

ABC Corp—just Bob Smith, "VP of Please Listen to Me, just because…"

See through the smoke to become an "entrepreneur," for what it truly means. Facing and enduring rejections and failures. No time with family; no leaving at five, six, or seven o'clock in the evening for dinner at home. Struggling. Selling 24-7. Patience, patience, patience, while constantly waiting for others to make up their minds. Constant stress and restlessness. Very little sleep. Tuning everyone else out, shutting your ears when people say you can't do it. No stable paycheck. No vacation time. No bonuses; no structured and promised yearly raises. Most importantly, years of very hard work before even the slightest results pop up.

If your heart is still screaming that you must take this on, then it's in your blood. The greatest test comes when your heart is still screaming to continue down this entrepreneurial path after a few failures. If this smoking gun of a bullet is truly lodged in your heart, without much fear to tackle whatever you are dealt, you have no choice but to join the entrepreneurial crowd. Welcome to roller-coaster hell and wondrous ongoing enlightenment in overcoming obstacles. And the best is yet to come: the incredible feeling of creating jobs for others, giving the world something new, living a life that is fulfilling for you, solving problems—all this while becoming more self-aware through every experience.

3. BE LIKE A CHAMELEON

Imitating and emulating successful leaders and entrepreneurs doesn't mean you lose your inner voice. Becoming what the situation or circumstance requires will allow you to learn positive behaviors of those around you. Being a chameleon is being flexible in my mind. It means you improve by listening and observing—in learning from those around you. I spend time observing leaders I admire. I was a right hand to four successful CEOs who were also entrepreneurs, each with their own leadership styles, convictions, successes, and past failures.

I simply absorbed. I observed how they spent time in the office, how they handled calls, at lunch and dinner, and I stayed late. I studied how they handled their teams, asked to join meetings (where I didn't really belong), and saw how they negotiated. When I went home, I practiced on my family. (Be pleasantly surprised how successful behaviors are transferable in managing home and personal-life issues.)

I feel I was born an entrepreneur, born to pave my own way. Many rejections, public criticisms, age and sex discrimination, twists and turns in my career as well as crumpled papers with ideas on them would prove just that. I believe this fire in your belly starts early, although you may not feel recognize it until later. I felt mine at age eighteen, perhaps even earlier. This fire in my belly came through even when I was trying to conceal it but it became increasingly uncomfortable to conceal; sometimes self-awareness sneaks up on you, and puts you face-to-face with who you are.

From what I have experienced, entrepreneurship can start and stop many times, before you truly embrace it as an integral part of your true self. I started businesses at a pretty early age without knowing what it meant to manage a business. I did that again and again, snuck into the corporate game, and then came back to my true self again.

Once, when I interviewed for an executive-assistant role, after a few interview rounds the CEO asked, "Why are you here?" I was shocked. He told me I was too smart to be his assistant; instead, I should be somewhere else telling people what to do. I told him I'd do just that if he hired me. He did. Entrepreneurs have an aura and a vibe about them that most other people notice. This CEO saw in me a person who isn't very well suited for rules, authority, and structures—even in a short conversation. Even as I helped him in this position, I was able to showcase my entrepreneurial abilities by bringing many changes, not only to his office but the organization as a whole. He allowed me to work as I wanted and empowered me to tackle decisions and bring in new initiatives. If he hadn't allowed me to work in this manner, I wouldn't have lasted, as the entrepreneurial bug usually keeps biting until you face it, and react accordingly.

As his right-hand assistant, I learned and mimicked behaviors people only hope to learn in their lifetimes. I fought these traits even as I adopted them. I wanted to prove these were not behaviors leading me to become successful. However, I learned and imitated them over time. He was the last CEO I worked for. I was recharged, surrounded with key people willing to help me build a strong leadership-foundation toolkit. I dove back into another business.

STAYING CLOSE TO POWER

However, the fire in my belly intensified back with the first CEO I worked for. I was in my early twenties, with zero assistant experience. I e-mailed him directly because his HR manager said she would get back to me after narrowing down candidates. She never did, and it wasn't acceptable for me. I wrote to this CEO that he'd be missing out if he didn't interview me. (Actually, I'd be the one missing out.) For a high-level leader in his industry, he responded to my e-mail fast. I found out later why he had so much time on his hands.

This CEO's giant glass office overlooked his entire company. (People kept looking over while I was there.) He was eating an apple, asked if I wanted one, and showed me a bag full of granny smiths (a habit I've since adopted, but that's not the lesson here).

He asked me why I wanted to be his assistant. Intuitively, I replied, "I want to be near power." I'll never forget those words.

They continue to be my life's theme. As I became more self-aware, I recognized that this theme kept resonating strongly in my consciousness. I was very honest with myself.

Once I realized what I said, I corrected it: "I mean, I want to help someone successful and powerful achieve their goals" (which was also true and continues to be).

"You're going to help me achieve my goals?" he asked. He smirked a little.

"Yes, and after only speaking to you for a few minutes, I know you'll help me achieve mine too," I replied.

He smiled. He said I could help him achieve one of his goals right then, turning around his computer screen. "Pick a vacation for me," he said. (I wanted to ask why he was looking for vacations at two o'clock in the afternoon on a workday in a glass office.) I saw gorgeous pictures of beaches and luxurious hotels. I immediately thought about everything I'd read up on him outside of his work accomplishments. I remembered he was athletic and adventurous. I blurted out, "Machu Picchu." The last thing this guy looked like he wanted to do was sit on a beach or sip cappuccinos in Paris.

What was the lesson he taught me at that first meeting (my biggest leadership lesson up to that point)? He gave me a chance; he asked me to come in. He didn't judge my experience or lack of it. He didn't judge the book by the cover. He didn't follow protocol (this resonated with me most). He didn't consult anyone on his team, which can be seen either as good or bad. He took the route that on paper would likely fail. I admired that bold move. He hired someone with no experience and knew nothing about his industry.

I admired the way he handled my interview (not because he hired me). I admired his ability to go against the grain, in trusting his gut instinct. He was an entrepreneur—a leader. I was lucky to learn leadership tactics from him that I continue to apply with my client teams today.

The reason he had so much time on his hands was another one of my lessons. *He hired the best people who operated his business without his constant intrusion.* This could be a dangerous lesson because for this tactic to work out well, people you hire must be bright and capable. They absolutely must have the company's best interests at heart. They must be loyal and devoted to the success of the company, and well matched to professional skill sets needed for the roles they perform.

4. ALIGNMENT IS KEY

I've mentioned why it's vital to be aligned with good leaders, to be able to observe and learn from them. Here is an example of why alignment is also critical for your success as an entrepreneur—to be in alignment with making smart business moves.

Michael, who was a wonderful accountant watched for years as his clients bought and sold increasingly larger properties. He called some clients to form an investment fund to purchase a commercial property. He partnered with some private investors of various backgrounds, ages and wealth, and asked if any of my clients or contacts wanted to join (a question I often get, in working with high net-worth people).

As an entrepreneur myself, I saw this wide range of people with different positions in life with different motivations, not to mention different disposable incomes, as "Misalignment 101." His investment team included eleven individuals (some very wealthy individuals, some retirees, some paying off their grandchildren's education, some saving for retirement, and other younger, motivated riskier investors). These individuals were very misaligned sitting in this melting pot. Some of these investors would likely want to flip this property with a quick turn, and others may be interested in a slow and steady growth with dividends and perhaps consider new acquisitions long term. This looked like a disaster to me. The reason I was privy to this misalignment was because I attended their investor meetings as the eyes and ears for possible new investors. Words from an incredible mentor rang in my ears every time I was listening to them speak about this partnership.

"Misaligned investors derail company potential. Make sure everyone is aligned in their investment strategy and goals for outcomes—always," my mentor advised. This classic advice has helped me coach entre- preneurs who thank me for warning them about possibly mismatched deals.

Back to Michael's story. His commercial property started out run- ning reasonably well. Michael loved to wag his finger at me, "I told you so." However, a few of the investors who held the major- ity investment found a buyer in their network after a few months and felt it was too cumbersome to manage with all its operational issues.

Aside from alignment, another lesson here is that real-estate prop- erties need time to generate decent cash flows. I learned this from working for large and small real-estate investment trusts (REITs). It takes time to improve the current operation from previous operators. It takes capital to turn around real-estate properties. Another dear friend and mentor taught me this. "You need to take a step back, see what changes need to be made, prioritize them, then brace yourself because it takes a long time to get real-estate properties operating successfully again," he said.

Clearly, in Michael's story, the investors did not give their property adequate time to be successful. Who ended up suffering? Smaller individual investors looking for portfolio growth and long term benefits. Today, Michael remains an accountant, focused on maintaining his professional status, which suits him to the core—focused on providing brilliant support for his clients because this is where his strength lies.

I don't mean to imply that career professionals cannot become entrepreneurs or operate their own investments; I know many who are successful having done just that. If that fire in you is strong, do the following:

- ✓ Get familiar with all of the issues a new entrepreneur faces in the first few years.
- ✓ Surround yourself with the right resources in your foundational toolkit to prepare you for the world of venturing out on your own.
- ✓ Align your business goals and strategies with people you care to work with.
- ✓ Look back one more time to understand what you are leaving behind and what you are about to face.

✓ Dig deep into self-awareness; what are your skills and natural abilities suited for?

LIZ'S TIPS FOR HONING YOUR LEADERSHIP AND ENTREPRENEURIAL EDGE

- Check your blood and your passion; are effective leadership and entrepreneurship coursing through your veins?
- Check how aligned partnerships, projects, and collaborations are.
- Build a strong foundation and keep your foundation toolkit handy.
- Ask for help, and get the right people invested in you and your success.
- Watch and listen. Absorb everything you can from successful and influential people.

Chapter 3

● ● ●

USING POLITICAL AWARENESS TO ACHIEVE OBJECTIVES

*They want to see you do good, but never
better than them...remember that.*

—A BRONX TALE

WHAT IS POLITICAL AWARENESS?

Being politically aware is to tune in to unspoken and indirect strategic influences that occur behind the scenes in every organization. Being politically savvy is an essential skill for leading effectively, in every area of corporate operations. Many naturally politically aware leaders refer to political savvy as common sense.

However, they don't realize it's not a very common trait; that many people have to learn this skill to maneuver around bureaucracy and other executives in order to influence those they need to influence, and to work productively in groups with other people.

It is vital to once again understand the concept of alignment pertaining to this context. Alignment is one of the primary leadership concepts I emphasize in this book. Being in alignment is to be aware of all the powerful forces that shape situations having an impact on people's lives (and just as applicable on the home and other interpersonal fronts, too).

I have also been guilty of calling political savviness and its skillful applications "common sense." And I learned over time I'd taken advantage of this fact (in my unsuspecting ignorance), that being politically savvy came naturally to me. I could not distinguish where my common sense stopped—and where being political savvy began. I recognize this natural quality in some clients as well, and need to remind them that this skill isn't natural for many people. I've watched over the course of my career changes, and in consulting experiences, how numerous great organizational ideas and changes fail, from a person's political power and influence.

Political waters are deadly if you step on toes, or swim against the current in forgetting to run certain things by certain people.

This is why the first tip below, about positive politics, is very important to understand, cultivate, and nurture. So are the other points, because they all work in tandem to becoming functional in developing your political savviness. Use them well, as you harness your talent in getting to, and staying put, at the top.

EIGHT CORE PRINCIPLES AND TRAITS OF POLITICAL AWARENESS

- Understanding why, and how, agreements occur.
- Knowing who the real decision-makers are, and *who* influences them.
- Knowing how to increase your visibility by participating in informal gatherings.
- Being aware of influencers' key motivations and agendas.
- An ability to prioritize key influencers' agenda in order to promote your own.
- Building alliances with those in power (not just those with positional titles).
- Anticipating shifts in power and planning for contingencies.
- Understanding key roles played by key people, and using this knowledge to achieve goals.

TIPS FOR IMPROVING POLITICAL AWARENESS

Some successful people lack the technical skills required for their jobs—yet possess the amazing ability to maneuver people and circumstances due to their political awareness. I am not suggesting you don't need talent and skill to succeed. I always have and will encourage a strong foundation. However, understand this: once you start swimming in political waters (the higher you go, the more politically infested the waters become with warring sharks and snarky strategies), the tougher it is to bring only skill and talent to the table. Why?

At a more advanced stage of junior leadership, you need to be liked and promoted by powerful and influential people who are invested in your continued professional successes. People who are bigger fish swimming in these waters must want to allow your capabilities to shine and surge forth—without the desire to drown you. Again, it pays to develop awareness, of self and of others.

LIZ'S TOP TEN TIPS TO BECOMING POLITICAL SAVVY

1. DEVELOP A GENUINE APPROACH TO APPRECIATING THE POWER OF POSITIVE POLITICS

Realize that cultivating political savviness in the office or any group setting is necessary; and react to it authentically. Once you understand that playing positive offense can be based on ethical standards, politics does not become negative. In fact, being adroitly aware of your environment and reacting to it in intelligent, reflective, and caring ways will bring light to illumine and heal from darkness that has been festering or demoralizing company or group culture.

2. WATCH OUT, AND LISTEN FOR:

(a) where true power lies, and
(b) where power *shifts*.

Sometimes, that overriding power force shifts daily in an organization—and you need to be aware of those power shifts, and wherever they flow to. When people are constantly fighting for attention and recognition from the powerful, the influence shifts very often, even briefly. I once watched a very powerful executive whom everyone labeled "untouchable" having to fight to save his position when he found himself in the midst of a "gang up" by other executives. One day, power shifted from him to someone else and that person held the spotlight for a brief period. However, he was smartly aware of this momentary power shift, and ably regained his poise by aligning with the power of the moment, in not losing a beat.

Learn to identify people's agendas. What motivates them? What do they want? How are they trying to get there? Are they ethical and morally sound people—people you'd care to have your name associated with? Can you partner with them to become more effective to produce winning teams? Are you aligned in your general approaches and strategic goals?

As the saying goes, knowledge is power; and being clueless about these signs may result in costly repercussions.

KEY RED FLAGS

Here are the *key red flags* to scan regarding power shifts: who has it, who is striving for power, or who is hanging on by a thread. Do your best to figure out the culture you are working in by reading people and more importantly, learn how to best deliver and self-promote within that culture.

- ✓ Watch out for people turning their personal agendas into "common goals" for the department or company; and worse, in getting away with it as they continue their rise to the C-suite.
- ✓ Watch for managers or supervisors preventing collaborations from taking place; ask yourself why this one person doesn't want the other two managers to collaborate.

✓ Watch for people using "powerful body language" in order to dominate conversations and get others to agree with their views—mainly from using body language that intimidates and with a louder, more strident voice. Believe too, that they are also doing this in the CEO's office or with other powerful executives.

✓ Watch for power plays with e-mails written in a certain tone, who they are copying (and also those who might be blind-copying), to make a powerful point or statement to whomever they are e-mailing. Don't forget that sometimes e-mails are written deliberately to make a point that would be recorded—yet the real communication happens on the phone or via text messages right after the e-mail was sent. For example, "Ignore that! I needed it to be on the record; so yes, go ahead with your proposal." Be aware of every possibility, of situations and people who are "not as advertised."

✓ Watch for the informal, indirect "yes-man syndrome."

✓ Watch for execs and managers who take up time with talking a lot, but really saying nothing. More significantly, watch if the CEO/power person accepts this approach as "normal and effective."

✓ Watch whole departments. Who seems relaxed? Whose department has it easier due to the power of that executive?

✓ Search for "the adviser." Who has the CEO/Power's ear? Advisers change often, so keep watching.

✓ Search for "the protector" acting as guard dog for the CEO/Power. Usually he or she hasn't nominated him- or herself for this understated and silent role; it was an unspoken assumption that he or she would keep his or her ears to the ground to help protect the CEO.

✓ Search for "the manipulator" trying to manipulate his or her way in—stay away from this person. Do not align with him or her at all costs; he or she will eventually be exposed.

✓ Look around for those who are "sticking by each other" and defending each other in front of the CEO/Power, and having each person's back. There may or may not be a covert reason for this.

3. UNDERSTANDING LEVERAGE FOR POWER POSITIONING

Organizations are power hierarchies. From time to time, the play of power shifts. To succeed, you need to know where opportunities for leverage lie; that is, who is influential at that moment. Often, powerful influence is informal (meaning it's not an influence that's easy to detect). It's only from watching out for it will you stay in tune with how these people influence others; for instance, perhaps in the form of a suggestion after a particular success. People who are politically aware know they hold the upper leverage for a very short time while the spotlight is on them. Be aware of who doesn't hold sway in the flow of power. How much power do you have yourself? Politically savvy people understand "the power of leverage concept" and can astutely recognize when it may be changing.

4. YOU CANNOT AVOID AND STAY AWAY FROM CORPORATE POLITICS

You *must* understand that staying out of "dirty politics" can actually hurt you in the corporate world. You must keep on playing the game and in keeping up with it. The added advantage in learning about it early on is that it helps you stay aware and on top of all your worlds—not just work. Learning to notice subtle changes and shifts in power is helpful to life on all fronts (including physical and emotional health symptoms).

Erin Burt, a career coach, advises, "Avoiding (office) politics altogether can be deadly for your career. Every workplace has an intricate system of power, and you can—and should—work it ethically to your best advantage" (lifehacker.com). I advocate this strategy because no news of office politics is bad news for you. Being astute and aware can only enhance your chances for professional success every step of the way.

Research by the Center for Creative Leadership (ccl.org) showed that those who were politically savvy had better career prospects, better career trajectories, and were seen to be more promotable. As with everything, you need to find a balance in being "aware of your surroundings"—and be careful not to cross into "brown-nosing" where you cannot stand to look in the mirror because you are no longer yourself. Even if you are not a power climber, not motivated by recognition, money, and power—and all you want to do is to keep your comfortable job—you must master office politics simply to keep your job, and not get blindsided or knocked off by other people's power plays.

5. UNDERSTAND THAT TO PARTNER WITH POWER, THE RELATIONSHIP *MUST* BE MUTUALLY BENEFICIAL

It's rare that people do something for absolutely nothing. Even those who relish the feeling of giving also feel good about themselves while giving of themselves (it is just not possible to be humanly, completely, and unconditionally selfless). You must offer something to the person you are trying to influence or partner with. There must be a reason for them to want to align with you or promote you, so give them opportunities to help them advance as well.

One thing that has worked for me every time and those I coach is, figuring out how to make others benefit from something you've done—and making them look good as a result of that action. However, most of the incredibly bright young people I coach want to stand out ASAP. They are so eager to have the light shine on them, in announcing they completed that important project or achieved that remarkable result.

Why do I advise against that? Because my golden rule is this:

If you stay in the shadows for the next twelve months delivering something for a powerful person, you can spend the rest of your career in the spotlight.

To start with, figure out what the influencers or powerful people need, and get it done for them. Do they need someone to help out on a project? Do they need someone to show up at a charity event they support and do the grunt work for free? Are you aware of a personal issue they are experiencing and could lend a hand bringing something over if they needed a cooked meal for their kids? *Standing out as the person who will go that extra mile for this influential individual (and who can eventually help you) is key.*

Another key approach is to ensure you're doing this without shining a spotlight on your activities. Do not tell anyone you are doing these things to help this person. If you don't share with others, the person you're helping will notice and appreciate your selflessness. Resist the desire to brag. Resist the desire to announce that you are the chosen one. This understated approach can only help your case. This cannot come from taking on a brown-nosing attitude. You must be genuine—to offer your assistance based on possibly *zero returns*. This has to come from a place that intuitively understands your actions may lead nowhere—but you are still happy to do it.

When people notice you leading consistently, powerful results will appear and accrue, including the following:

- ✓ You start inspiring trust, which is key to influencing others.
- ✓ You get involved in something personal with them (giving you something to share in common, that is apart from what others have to offer).
- ✓ You become the indirect "go-to" for this person(s).
- ✓ This person starts speaking about you to other influencers—who begin to notice you when you walk by; perhaps even ask you to get involved in other projects based on good reviews from the initial influencer.

6. YOU NEED TO COMMIT TO THE ORGANIZATION 100 PERCENT

You need to give it your loyalty, your interest, and your genuine desire for the organization's success—which will be noticed. When you commit to the company, your genuine interest in understanding the entire business (not just your area) naturally expands. Most employees are not committed to the business and instead are committed to their jobs and paychecks, advancement, and personal recognition. Not too often are people truly committed to the success of their entire organization, on all levels.

Even more remarkable, when you commit 100 percent of your positive energies, you start thinking horizontally instead of vertically. Incredibly, a magical transformation occurs. Horizontal thinkers are those with the ability to understand and see the functionality of other departments, how various departments either help or hinder each other. As you commit to the company's success, you start noticing areas outside of your responsibility and start coming up with genuine ways to improve relevant initiatives as you see them—from your enhanced vision.

Once you get this deeply involved on a personal level, with the promise of providing a workable vision for the business to succeed and prosper, power starts coming to you. People will notice your dedicated commitment not only to your job but also to the company's overall profitability—and this truly makes you a standout to influencers.

Influencers (assuming they are positive influencers) are also people who are truly committed to doing their best for the business to thrive and succeed. Why? Because when the business thrives, everyone is in on a winning team.

7. YOU CANNOT RELY ON CHARISMA AND CHARM

Many people think that being politically wise has much to do with interpersonal skills. In fact, many people rely on their charm to get by in politically charged environments. They rely on their charm offensives so much that it ironically hinders their progress toward developing real strategies to influence and advance in an organization—in other words, they are shooting their own feet with purposeless words and actions that less astute people readily swallow. Being charming can help, but there needs to be substance behind every action; otherwise, you will not be considered for serious results-focused tasks.

8. GATHER A TEAM, SPREAD YOUR INFLUENCE, AND SAY GOOD-BYE TO THE VICTIM STATUS

A key tactical offense in playing office politics and trying to stay politically aware is knowing who is around you—meaning you must refresh your circle of people. As I mentioned before, you are much stronger when supported by others, even if that support and trust comes from your level or levels below. Feeling protected and trusted within your area or department is a very good tactic to feel empowered and supported when dealing with and facing senior staff and influencers.

When you start influencing your own people or team before you even put your hat in the leadership race, you will be noticed just for leading without a title. This is much tougher to achieve than positional leadership where a title has to be given to you. You need to first gather the support of your peers and then climb the ladder with that much more support. This helps you immensely in staying politically aware—and relevant. That's because those who trust you to lead them, and support you most of the time, are very willing to share information with you; which in turn empowers you even more.

Many people complain that they cannot change or affect situations positively that they see as unfair or ineffective. Many people like to play "the victim" as it gives them reasons to sit back and do nothing but complain to others. Look around your workplace (and family), and you'll spot these self-inflicted victims right away; a large part of their attitude enjoys this "status."

Lawrence Cheok's "7 Habits to Win in Office Politics" identified Habit #3 as "Focus on Your Circle of Influence." Cheok found that having influence over your circle gives you control, instead of a changing corporate environment that is beyond anyone's control. This "is a very empowering technique to overcome the feeling of helplessness and shows those around you that you know how to operate around constraints," and concluded, "instead of feeling victimized, focus on what you can do to influence a salutation—your circle of influence" (life-hack.org).

9. WATCH OUT; IT HAPPENS BEHIND THE SCENES

Some clients tell me they are lucky to work for nonpolitical environments, that there are not too many political machinations where they work. This makes me laugh, because I know then my client is completely clueless of what's going on behind the scenes. Why? Because, most insider politics happen out of view of everyone else's knowledge of what is overtly happening.

Leaders rarely expose their intimate agenda publicly. How so? Because, when most employees leave work between after five or six o'clock in the evening, the political-insider game begins. Besides, developing political awareness is like developing a sixth sense that functions at a different frequency. In order to truly be aware of it, you need to elevate to that frequency.

10. HOW DECISIONS ARE MADE AND WHO MAKES THEM

I know enough leaders to know that many important decisions aren't made by people high on the organizational chart or along the chain of command. In reality, there are various people contributing to important decisions that affect your workplace and often—you. Hence, it pays to study your environment, to try and spot who these influential folks are. They're usually part of the "old boys/girls club." (I don't mean they're older or that they hold executive positions.)

Such informal power circles are very difficult to penetrate because people have gained unofficial memberships, and they continue to have influence and sway decision making by giving opinions. Opinion-making-and-giving often continues outside the office, at a dinner, or any outside function. It's important to be aware of who these individuals are. Even though it might take you longer to penetrate and look inside, staying close to key unofficial members will help you get a clearer idea on how decisions are made, and who has a hand in influencing them.

After a few years of sitting at management-team tables, I now ask myself at these meetings *who isn't at this meeting today, who should be here?* I have been in that chair long enough to know that the assistant sitting outside the CEO's office may have more influence than many others sitting at the table next to the CEO. Real brainstorming often takes place not at the leadership-team table—but at a golf game or a private conversation during a business trip. I once witnesses an acquisition decision be confirmed after two CEO wives went to lunch. Understanding this dynamic exists can give you immense power and leverage to play your hand in positive and ethical ways.

When you've assessed who the key players are (and often it makes little sense), then I am confident you are on track to conquering the political world at your workplace. Understand this: if you're outside this network, you cannot influence decision making. You can only react to a key decision only after it has been made. Thus, getting closer to individuals you think can influence those decisions (while at the same time trying your best to make senior leaders realize you understand this power-play dynamic) is key to eventually becoming one of these influential individuals and power brokers yourself.

BONUS: IN THE END, ETHICS WIN

Being politically aware and playing the game doesn't have to have a negative connotation—always remember this. Political agendas can be very ethical; you don't need to overtly manipulate for your personal gain. The agenda must suit the business as a whole, not just your own desires. Although it takes time, manipulative and explosive players are often exposed. Especially when power shifts away from them on to someone else; when they can no longer hide behind "being liked" or "having the boss's ear." When your day comes, the more ethical and fair you have been in your approach, the fewer backlashes there will be.

WHAT DOES IT TAKE TO BE POLITICALLY SAVVY?

Self-awareness along with the following:

- ✓ Determination to persevere while facing extreme challenges
- ✓ Resourcefulness and resilience
- ✓ Reflection before action
- ✓ Becoming an ever-faster learner in picking up nonverbal signs
- ✓ Composure, or poise and grace under fire
- ✓ Compassion and sensitivity
- ✓ Respecting differences of opinions
- ✓ Ability to adapt quickly in alignment with others and situations
- ✓ Trustworthiness and reliability

BE CREDIBLE AND VISIBLE

In the corporate world, you need both performance and political savviness. You not only need to work hard to produce results and credibility—but also work equally hard (even harder) to establish your visibility. Credibility exists when your productive output meets approval and endorsement, and other positive factors support your results and productivity. Visibility happens when your work is continuously recognized and endorsed by the right individuals.

Combining the two vital keys of credibility and visibility will enhance your political position immensely—and bring you closer to individuals of influence (both formal and informal). When people look up to you, and notice you as a result of your credible standing, along with endorsements by key people promoting your visibility, you are truly winning the power game and have become a winning influence yourself.

LIZ'S TIPS FOR USING POLITICAL AWARENESS TO ACHIEVE OBJECTIVES

- Accept that office politics exists and find a way in, ethically.
- Use only ethical tactics within politically charged environments.

- Find influencers around you who do not always have impressive titles.
- Be aware of shifting power surges; the waters change often.
- Inspiring trust will often get you closer to positions of influence.

Chapter 4

* * *

TOP TEN PERSUASION TIPS LEADERS MUST CULTIVATE

*If you wish to win a man over to your
ideas, first make him your friend.*

—ABRAHAM LINCOLN

SEEK TO HEAR AND TO UNDERSTAND: A PATHWAY TO PERSUASION

I have been called *strategic* by others who meant it in a negative sense. To me, strategic isn't a negative word. It means understanding peoples motives, thought processes, and emotional drivers. My strategy is and has always been to hear what someone is saying and also what they are *not* saying. My strategy has *always* been to understand, because it is through understanding that I am able to see how to position my advice to clients in a way that they will find enlightening. I align with those I seek to persuade.

Ultimately, understanding people's motivations underscores the significant need to be in alignment with them. Understanding the concept of *alignment is key* to empower you with successful leadership. To successfully influence and persuade others, you must win over their hearts and minds. People are more agreeable with those who have touched them, who make them feel understood.

Most people want to be heard and to be understood. Strive to understand the other people's reasoning for ideas and choices they present and make. Understanding a person's reasoning is a powerful persuasion tool.

Ask questions to figure out *what's* behind their opinions; even trying to understand their more casual choices helps. Such as, why did they choose to sit where they did? Why did they accept or decline certain invitations? Why did they bring a friend or direct report from their old company with them to their new position? What *emotion* is behind these decisions?

When you learn their reasoning behind action and decision, you can inspire them to think about your point of view by using logical arguments to support the way their thought processes work. If you use their unique reasoning or the emotional that sits behind it and mimic their thought processes to make your argument inspiring in addition to making sense for them, they'll generally agree with you—and often, perhaps not that very instant but the seed will be planted in the right place. The key here is to first get a clear picture and study how they frame their thoughts and more importantly, what emotions are behind those thought processes. Some of the more prevalent emotions behind decisions are: fear, security, recognition and acceptance.

I coach my clients not to lead with facts alone when supporting their views. People don't often respond well to just data, without an emotional connection. You're better off leaving everything open to the person you're trying to influence. After learning how to reason your way toward making them feel they're heard by you, they'll invariably reflect upon your reasoning. Just leave them alone after stating your emotionally connected point of view; they'll seek you out later to continue the discussion.

DIFFERENT PERSUASION STYLES

After years of observing clients and mentors in action, three effective styles of persuasion, influence, and negotiation, stand out.

1. Silence is golden.
2. Wield your power.
3. Keep most of your farm.

1. SILENCE IS GOLDEN

People who are eager to persuade often impatiently and anxiously await responses from those they are trying to influence. Erroneously, they think that silence means the need for them to give more facts, examples, and reasons to bolster their proposition. In my experience, most of the time silence is the most powerful point of persuasion and negotiation.

Power doesn't simply lie in silence itself. The exchange after the period of silence is of equal importance; it can completely diminish the power of silence if you continue to persuade—post silence. One of my incredibly intelligent sponsors and friends, George, took me to a meeting 10 years ago. At this meeting he tried to persuade a man he often does business with, to agree to his view. Upon reaching a silence threshold, George spoke first. But, what he said had nothing to do with the business at hand; George simply asked the other person how his winery was doing (he had just bought a small winery in France).

They talked about the winery, and soon after parted ways. There was no decision made. I asked George what had been decided; he said he was sure this gentleman would take his directive. I asked him how he was so sure and he said, "I'm giving him time to see that my way is the best way. What else is there to say?"

George wasn't worried at all. I kept thinking how much more he could have said in his argument to push the man closer to his point of view and examples he could have given; but he didn't need them; he had a quiet assurance about him, his style didn't require anything extra. He was right; this man came back with various reasons on why George's way was the right way. He was the one to reach out first, after George gave him the time needed to reflect wisely.

Avoid the temptation to speak again, especially soon after you've made a powerful point; you will likely dilute your powerful point if you continue speaking. Allow the point to "brew." I've watched talented clients in negotiations; many understood this persuasion tactic. They were silent after expressing what they needed to express. Silence eventually drove the other person to speak—which usually weakened their position. Don't appear desperate; take a step back long enough to get your way.

Power Tip: Let silence prevail.

2. LEARN TO WIELD YOUR POWER

I sat in a boardroom with one of my clients a few years back. This man is aggressive, but he's not verbally aggressive; something about his presence makes you feel a little intimidated. He presents himself in a very powerful way through his calm and assertive demeanor; his image means a great deal to his staff in wielding his power. He may not know this but watching him, I was able to define something I have been doing naturally since a young age. My client had listed one of his large real-estate properties and wanted the deal done right, quick, and for top dollar. We sat waiting for the broker, who came in looking powerful and presentable, as my client did.

Once the broker sat down, they started discussing the property. I've had other clients list similar major real-estate properties and understood the details to be there as a resource for my client. I was also familiar with the staff at that particular property, having trained them every quarter to operate it more effectively, and knew exactly what the buyer would be getting if he or she purchased it. To me, this property as well as the people who worked there, were special.

Little did I know; my client had no specific skill for negotiation that people can read up on. I was awestruck by the impressive reasoning he used to persuade the broker to lower his fees, increase the price for the property, plus ten other stipulations the broker would have to accept if he wanted my client's listing. The broker kept throwing out mutually beneficial solutions, which I understood and endorsed.

Each time, my client responded with *no*, followed by a deafening silence. With each *no*, the broker was forced to rethink and produce another solution to be acceptable to my client. The broker continued doing that over and over again—until he reached a position where my client finally said, "Perhaps, keep going." I was excited; *no* had turned into "perhaps." However, the broker felt he needed to give more.

Upon reaching the silence stage, the broker did just that—he produced a solution whereby my client received almost everything he had initially wanted, leading my client to respond, "I think I can work with that." It wasn't even a *yes*. I didn't see any excitement in my client's face even after receiving almost everything he'd asked for.

Silence after a strong response is powerful. It signaled to the broker to speak, just as in my first tip. When you're signaled to speak, you're compelled to say something different from the previous statement that had received a *no*. Thus, you habitually present another scenario simply because you're working toward a *yes*.

I'm not suggesting this approach will work often or for most people. It's what's *behind* this approach that is very effective; namely, the determination to wield power by risking loss—to gain what you want from the other side. I believe every negotiator and persuader marks a line that represents how much they're willing to let go of, and to lose. My client's line that day was solid, while the broker's was very flexible. This won't be the case every time; apply it to your own circumstance.

Power Tip: Assess where the power line lies for the person you're trying to influence, and then wield your power.

3. KEEP MOST OF YOUR FARM

Giving away too much makes people want less (and you appear less desirable to agree to). I have worked with people in charge of sales departments and have needed to sell myself on occasion. Selling is a big part of almost all jobs. I sell as a mom, wife, speaker, trainer, adviser, and coach. I'm constantly selling people to consider things, reflect on things, and make various suggestions I would like my clients to adopt. (I also sell broccoli to my kids.) We all sell, all the time, many without a sales title. What I have learned over the years working closely with top-notch sales executives and trying to sell myself is, *adding more sugar to the deal makes people reassess what they're getting.*

I watch some of my younger clients trying to sell themselves, who often undervalue themselves in negotiations, in giving away the farm. To clarify, I support this concept at the beginning of your career as you are still building up. However, when you give away everything, you often become less desirable. Once you cross that line, people start looking at your product or service as common, cheap, and not useful. Worse, they look at you that way.

People generally need to feel *they* (and they alone) are getting a super deal—but not too much of a good deal. People need to feel they're getting *value* but that what they're buying isn't *cheap*. It's a *big* difference in perception between value and cheap.

Selling is a big part of influence and persuasion. When you're trying to get someone to see your point of view or to get behind you, don't give him or her too much, or he or she won't want that deal after all. This is also true when you're up against someone more powerful and in a better position to leverage. Giving away too much when trying to persuade just communicates you had started weaker (even if that's true, do not act like it is).

In their book *YES: 50 Scientifically Proven Ways to Be Persuasive* (2010), Noah Goldstein, Steve Martin, and Robert Cialdini ask, "When does a bonus become an onus?" They discussed social scientist Priya Raghubir's hypothesis: *when consumers are offered a bonus gift for purchasing a product, the perceived value and desirability of the bonus gift will sharply decline with the initial offer.* Raghubir suspected this was the case when consumers felt the manufacturer would not give away something valuable freely; that people would start asking, "What's wrong with this deal?" Raghubir's experiment evaluated the cost of a piece of jewelry given to them along with a free gift, against another group that purchased just the jewelry. Her findings showed people were willing to pay 35 percent less when they saw it bundled with a free gift—than if they were willing to pay for it as a standalone item.

Power Tip: To avoid devaluing your advice, point of view, or service, stop overselling.

DEVELOPING PERSUASIVE PRESENTATIONS FOR BUY-INS

Influence and persuasion are necessary when presenting new ideas and projects to be received positively; and in getting others to work with you. Below are tips in working toward positive outcomes to get people to join, or buy into your ideas.

1. REFLECT ON YOUR STRATEGIC APPROACH; MAKE SURE THE IDEA IS GOOD

Do not wing your approach to colleagues, bosses, or staff. Prepare your approach. Prepare for objections prior to going in to your presentation or meeting. Most of us intuitively know what the top three specific objections might be regarding our projects; prepare to combat them before you go in. Do whatever it takes; prepare to bring other people to the meeting; call someone while you are with this person, bring some stats from various reports, bring whatever you anticipate might be needed to combat objections.

2. BE PREPARED FOR A *NO*

One of the most powerful positions in a negotiation or persuasion is being prepared for a *no*. The best way to prepare for a *no* is to have a backup plan ready. Before meeting with the person you are trying to persuade, ensure you have spoken to a few others who are in alignment with your quest and could be possible replacements if the desired person says no. Starting these conversations before presenting to the person of interest will make you more at ease; this relaxed confidence is easily felt by the person you approach. It also takes the pressure off them to give you what you want—which ironically, often makes them give you exactly what you want. Always work with other options in the background; contingency planning is important prior to starting any venture, project, request, or opportunity.

3. ENSURE THAT THE PERSON YOU ARE APPROACHING FEELS THAT THIS REQUEST OR PRESENTATION IS SPECIFIC TO THEM

Start by making the individual you approach feel special and singling out this individual's team as preferred people you'd most like to collaborate with, for specific reasons (list these specific reasons). The way you begin will either kill or win the deal. You need to begin by appealing to the ego of the person you are approaching, not yours. That will grab his or her attention to listen to the rest. It's similar to asking for help; start with a compliment that explains why you're asking them specifically for their help. Explain why their help would stand out compared to others. (For example, in asking, "Your presentation was so appealing to the eye that you really captivated us! Would you mind offering suggestions for mine?")

This is a beneficial strategy to broach presentations in a similar way: single out with praise, show your genuine appreciation, highlight and compliment positives, and then present your case persuasively. Another powerful tactic when trying to get someone to align with you to join your project is to use the word "we" even before the person has agreed. Make the person picture this already happening. For example:

- ✓ "When you and I attack this thing"
- ✓ "When our teams actually get together"
- ✓ "You and I should strategize and definitely figure things out together before anything happens."

This approach makes the other person feel he or she's already agreed. Use "we" and "us" in positive ways throughout your presentation.

4. GIVE THEM A CHANCE TO SAY NO; SHOW RESPECT FOR THEIR TIME

Ask them about their projects. What is their staff busy with? Also, give them a chance to say no right there; ask if they're up against deadlines. Give them a chance to tell you they're too busy to take on another project for the moment. Offer to give them time to think. When you offer people time to think, they don't usually want it; they feel they'll lose out on something. (In this case, approach someone else and their team and they'll get the accolades.) The respect you show when offering time and a chance to say *no* gets you much farther. This colleague will see you as a person who respects and appreciates him or her and humanizes you in his or her eyes.

5. PUNCH—AFTER TIME-OUT

Once you give them a chance to say no, seduce them with positive points that will come about resulting from their cooperation. Talk about the opportunity for their team's exposure, an opportunity to advance skill sets, to take their team out of the mundane. Talk about another project that went extremely well in the company and what opportunities opened up for those individuals and the accolades they received. (For example, "Remember, Rebecca got that big promotion and was invited to that golf event after they competed project ABC?") When you do this after a "time-out" and show you are respectful and not desperate for their participation, these obvious facts don't seem "salesy" because they were said right after a period of indifference or rejection.

6. DO NOT OFFER MORE; OFFER JUST THE OPPOSITE—OFFER LESS

As I explained in my *tips for persuasion*, giving people more makes them suspicious. It makes you look desperate; they'll start wondering what's in this offer for them. The more they analyze the deal, the worse it becomes for you. Stay away from sentences, offers, and remarks that make them rethink the subconscious decision they've already made to say "yes" to you. People often push too far; they already had a "yes" from the other side and have them convinced with their subtle ways but then…they keep talking more, and ruin it all.

7. LEAVE, DON'T LOOK BACK, AND ASSUME THERE IS A DEAL

By now, if you still don't have a concrete agreement (most of the time you should), don't push. Leave assuming it's yours but don't ask the direct question. When you ask, you get an answer because the other person feels pressured to respond. Even as kids when we asked our parents direct questions, we often got a *no*. When you don't ask directly, you don't get an immediate *no*. Give your proposal or request a chance to brew and flourish, and walk away positively. Shake the person's hand, smile, convey a slight assumption that there is a deal, e-mail this person thereafter to thank him or her for his or her time, and convey your excitement in working with him or her.

LIZ'S TOP TEN PERSUASION TIPS FOR LEADERS (DO NOT CONFUSE WITH MANIPULATION.)

- Always get the support and endorsement of team members. Then mention it only at the end as a side note, as though you didn't intend for this nugget to come out. Name-dropping out of the gate and speaking about the support you have and who agrees with your ideas makes the person you're persuading fight your concept that much harder.

- Silence is golden; learn to make your point—then stop.

- The point you make after a very powerful point loses its value (thus, best not to make another point there and then).

- Hearing and understanding the other person's perspective and emotional drivers is essential to persuading them.

- As your credibility and endorsement value increases, so does your ability to persuade.

- Create a blog, comment on ideas; start influencing others outside your circles.

- Speak the same language as the person you are trying to persuade. Speak to his or her education level, nonprofit causes he or she supports, and his or her level of humor. Appeal to his or her confidence (not yours).

- Don't underestimate the power of uncertainty. Uncertainty may make people imagine a greater opportunity than reality. When people spend more time thinking about your message, it emboldens your idea with more impact. Give them useful nuggets to ponder.

- To persuade is to get them to "feel," not "think." Strive to create a valuable image and a deeper sense of feeling and in connecting with them.

- Don't generate a feeling in the person you're trying to persuade that makes him or her want to disagree for the sake of disagreeing. Some people become irritated with the way they're approached and spoken to; they'll just disagree no matter what you say. Adjust your tone and remove that car-salesman hat!

PART 2
SEEING THROUGH SMOKE

Chapter 5

●　●　●

LEADERS IN DENIAL AND BLIND SPOTS TO TACKLE

The speed of the human mind is remarkable.
So is its inability to face the obvious.

—SIMON MAWER

A HABIT POWERED BY FEAR

Some department heads, even CEOs, lead in denial. Denial about who surrounds them, denial about what their company looks like deep down, denial about the toxicity that may be taking over outside of their office doors. Denial is a habit mostly powered by fear. Fear of having to piece things together after digging deep. Fear of finding out what had occurred under their noses and fear of acknowledging that skilled and talented people are affected by the toxic behavior of others, thus giving up on the company or department. Some people are afraid to say and acknowledge the truth; leaders are no exception. The common underlying truth is—many people are not honest with who they are. Why does this happen?

The reasons for leading in denial are many. A primary reason is, leaders may be afraid to lose what they have built, or as it is perceived by others. No matter what their outer bravura, many people lack authentic security deep down inside. I know many leaders who are authentically secure and very self-aware; they behave very differently from the ones I know who have some insecurities deep down that affect their actions. As a result of their insecurities, some managers, directors, and vice presidents are afraid to develop others professionally, for fear of underlings making more professional progress than they themselves can muster. I see some of them backing away from brilliant ideas their team members present; instead, they highlight the qualities of those less skilled. Less talented team members present them with opportunities under the umbrella of wanting to "develop them"; they tread carefully around those truly talented, often effectively holding them back. I am not suggesting that all of this happens on the conscious level. I don't think many people out there purposely and vindictively like holding others back, but as a result of a deep rooted fear their actions sometimes suggest that.

People often seek and are driven by acknowledgment. People are more agreeable with those who have touched them, and who make them feel understood. Yet the irony is, rarely do people know and understand themselves first—let alone others and where others are coming from. I see many leaders making decisions that go directly against who they truly are. Sadly, when leaders are insecure and fearful, they fight their own truths and principles. Not surprisingly, while their fear intimidates others, they do *not* get much in terms of support and goodwill from those who they feel they have strongly invested in, their staff.

FEAR OF FACING REALITY

Facing reality takes a lot of work; it takes guts and an open mind to fix things that require fixing. Some people love to say, "If it isn't broken, don't fix it." If you're the one in denial, ask someone else (not a yes-man) if it is really working. There are many agendas and reasons for leaders of any level to continue operating within the smoke of denial. Why? Because it feels comfortable and familiar to not ruffle feathers.

Many know deep down that they must change and on some level are just stalling. They work hard to prevent certain truths from surfacing and for the most part keep "truth seekers" and "exposers" far away from them. Unluckily for them, they prefer to surround themselves with yes-men, people who won't challenge them often. Perhaps they are people so grateful for the opportunities they have been given that they continue to operate within the "yes" agenda, for fear of losing their opportunities, as they may not feel deserving of them deep down. Sometimes the reasons for these denials are political in nature. Leaders are afraid to dig deep for fear of what they might find festering away in departments they supposedly have expertise and insight on overseeing efficiently and effectively. A CEO, for example, may feel that digging for the truth does not produce positive results, thus allowing top executives to continue leading their teams in an unhealthy way. (After all, questioning these leaders puts the CEO's competence and leadership ability in question, as well; it is much easier not to ruffle feathers.)

Eventually though, the truth surfaces; these leaders are left with having to cope with much bigger messes than if they hadn't allowed the seductive draw of denial to seduce them in, in the first place. For the most part, it is easier to ignore red flags, not ruffle feathers, and *hope* things will miraculously change. Many people don't even consider change until their mess starts spilling over to where the public can see it and criticize it. Some leaders may subconsciously enjoy this dangerous, idyllic momentary space—the lull before the storm erupts. Human nature finds it more comfortable to coast along on an ocean free of storms and unsettling waves and motions—without having to deal with queasy seasickness.

Except that leaders need to understand that stormy seas and larger oceans do invariably crest when the weather changes—to culminate in stories being revealed, people talking, finger pointing, and executives finally getting exposed. Worse follows. Rebuilding morale and losing key team members in the process of rebuilding company culture are as daunting as in having to pick up the operational pieces again, while trying to maintain productivity and team harmony.

However, the good news is—leaders who are (a) self-aware, (b) keep their ears to the ground in communicating with their teams and informal influencers, plus (c) think long term strategically to anticipate and plan for contingencies don't typically allow a downward spiral to reach this devastating stage for their companies to hurt so badly. This strategy is critical to maintain as an ongoing preventative measure. This strategy needs to see through smoke that certain members of the team may be blowing.

LAYERING

The concept of *layering* is a subtle and Band-Aid strategy many leaders in denial engage in—with long-term repercussions for themselves and their companies. Layering occurs when a leader hires additional people to cover up for the job not optimally performed by the person hired to perform that job (who ought to be capable of handling it well, barring major task changes). Leaders, often in an attempt not to have to deal directly with the issue of incompetence, go on to hire additional people to help that key person more ably perform the role he or she was originally hired to undertake.

However, unless the job scope has changed immensely with numerous extra new responsibilities, there are no convincing reasons to layer on that role with new hires. Unless, of course, the top dog is trying to avoid digging into what is going on, or a department head has been convincing enough that extra hands on board are necessary to alleviate their pressures to meet deadlines. Leaders will find it pays to dig, to peel back layers, to find out what is festering away in that particular department or team.

Tag Goulet of Fabjob.com has listed ten reasons for layering in his article "Why bad employees don't get fired," published by *Career Builder* (2007) and online at CNN.com. Culpable reasons ranged from "the employee has a relationship with someone higher up," to "boss feels sorry for the employee,". In coaching leaders to unleash their fearlessness to accept and cope with ailing realities, I have found these reasons prevailing unnecessarily.

No matter what the reasons are, layering occurs often in organizations. I wholeheartedly encourage and strongly recommend that leaders get to the root of issues that need fixing. Leaders in denial on what needs to be accepted and transformed are similar to people denying that medical treatment is needed—thereby allowing a disease to continue festering in them. The sooner steps are taken to cut off the offensive head or source, the sooner will both people and companies heal, in returning to and maintaining longer-term good health.

LEADING WITH TRUST

I am blessed with some incredibly honest and self-aware clients; they inspire me daily. One client, who is a CEO of a mid-size company, knows exactly who he is—and what he needs to do to lead effectively and gain respect. Over our years working together, I see him making decisions every day that come from a very honest and authentically confident place.

This leader isn't "weak" or "soft"; neither can he be manipulated. He leads with integrity. He expects others to be honest with him. He sets an example by leading with respect. He does this so naturally and effortlessly, he receives team support seamlessly and abundantly from employees, vendors, and industry top dogs. Does this mean that there aren't times when he knows the wool was pulled over his eyes? No. Instead, he welcomes both positive and negative forces to surface—and to dig deeper for reasons to remedy what needs fixing. He is very equipped to deal with repercussions of digging in and finding out "the truth" for himself; he believes in his ability to rebuild and surrounds himself with other honest and confident leaders. You could say that other principled leaders naturally flock to him.

LEADERSHIP-DENIAL SIGNS

1. LEADERS WHO CONTINUOUSLY SEARCH FOR SOLUTIONS TO FIX EVERYTHING—BUT ARE UNCLEAR ABOUT WHAT NEEDS FIXING

Leaders who look at anything but themselves—outside of their thoughts and actions to fix issues—are unaware of how their personal habits invariably impact and affect those around them with their leadership styles. Leaders in denial look to the next management solution, consultant, or strategy as a way out, for magical cop-out solutions to fix everything—while stopping short of questioning their own actions that may have caused ripple effects to percolate down through the ranks, resulting in inadvertently cracking up the company's structure and operations. I can honestly say I have been on the other end of this phone call from some prospective clients. I have learned to distinguish between prospective clients who are looking for an outside solution and those who genuinely could benefit from third-party assistance and perspectives.

2. LEADERS WHO DO NOT ALLOW CONSTRUCTIVE OPPOSITION

Leaders in denial often suppress the views that disagree with their points of view. They regard disagreement or varying points of view as unhealthy. They sometimes label this feedback as lacking respect for their authority. A genuine leader, in wanting to achieve overall success, will do what it takes to move forward, even if it means hearing the negative perspectives and agreeing to revise plans.

3. LEADERS WHO ARE NOT OPEN TO LEARNING AND WHO LACK CURIOSITY

Leaders in denial fail to recognize the need for ongoing learning, of the value to consider new ideas and engage in continued learning. The seeds of failure are sown when leaders are closed to learning, are no longer willing to be vulnerable in order to learn, are no longer curious, and are unwilling to be challenged with exciting new ideas to transform and inspire with their dynamic leadership.

4. LEADERS WHO SUGARCOAT AILING REALITIES

Leaders in denial often sugarcoat current realities by putting positive spins on everything. However, being able to face reality ensures that leaders are honest in facing challenges that must be dealt with constructively. Leaders sometimes downplay ailing realities in attempts to protect people from facing more challenges, and from creating perceived unnecessary concerns. However, in my opinion, keeping employees too "safe" doesn't really help the business at all.

5. LEADERS STUBBORNLY FOLLOWING WHAT WORKED IN THE PAST (OR DIDN'T) AND ARE UNAWARE

This trap is one that leaders of successful organizations fall into regularly. Leaders continue to rely on strategies and tactics that have worked in the past. Or, if those strategies didn't work but were saved by other managers below them, never realizing it, and thus never learning from their failed strategies. Some organizations are more likely to deny new realities, because old realities had worked so well for them. Older and more established organizations tend to stubbornly stick with past habits, to deny new realities (that help them make constant progress while besting competition). Do you wonder why so many older businesses are struggling to keep up in light of newer ones that are ever ready to consider new strategic approaches to maintain their core competencies?

6. LEADERS WHO LAY BLAME ON EXTERNAL FACTORS OR ON OTHERS, FOR THEIR MISTAKES

The blame game is often used as a distraction to free leaders from the difficult task of having to face failing strategies. They often just *must* find someone to point the finger at. In looking for someone else to blame, it means leaders don't have to deal with those ugly situations. Yet, leaders need to courageously face these disappointing realities and not deflect blame onto others.

FIVE WAYS TO TACKLE LEADERSHIP BLIND SPOTS

1. DON'T HIRE IN YOUR IMAGE

Do your best to stay away from hiring people who mirror you because hiring people who are similar to your sensibilities may result in organizational weaknesses. Instead, focus on surrounding yourself with individuals who have skills and ideas complementing and strengthening your team's overall skill sets. You need to create a balance within the company to avoid blind spots and being sucked into making wrong decisions as a result of misinformation or simply not seeing through the smoke at creative new options to stay competitive.

2. ENCOURAGE YOUR TEAM MEMBERS TO SPEAK UP

A great way to combat blind spots is to ensure that your team isn't afraid to speak up. One client says she'd rather hear a long story about how something might potentially go wrong and waste everyone else's time—than make the team member feel too afraid to say anything which could lead to her making an error. If you hire people who complement your skills and are resourceful, they will often watch your blind spots for you—but only *if* you allow, enable, and encourage them to do so openly.

3. KNOW THYSELF AND THY HABITS

Do we truly understand our habits? Do we go over them with a fine-toothed comb? What are your habits? What comes to you naturally? How do you instinctively react to people and overwhelming situations? How do you process information? How do you analyze information in applying what you learned for strategic considerations? These are some questions that I ask my clients to consider in becoming more self-aware; some quickly realize that their own natural habits may be hidden from them.

Sometimes, blind spots are merely habits that can be resolved by paying attention to them, in altering them with new and untried ways. A useful tactic is to understand what and how your personal habits affect you. Ask questions such as the following:

- ✓ Am I a good listener?
- ✓ Am I missing, losing, or not registering what's being said after a brief time?

✓ Am I multitasking too much, to ably process lots of information all at one time?

✓ Do I have favorites on my team and tune out negative feedback on them?

✓ Am I patient with colleagues when they describe a problem or issue?

✓ Do I habitually feel someone else will handle the issue I'm being told about?

4. LOOK BACK AND REFLECT, TO MOVE FORWARD

Examine your history of decision making. When were the times you felt you missed something, didn't see something big that was waiting to explode? Examine what it was about your missing those danger signals; then reflect, dissect, and analyze what creative options could avoid making similar errors the next time round.

One glaring leadership lesson to learn is, *until we correct the underlying reasons behind an error, the error keeps repeating itself in one form or other.* Good reflections to consider are as follows:

✓ When we faced that issue previously, I wish I'd examined _____ better, before going forward.

✓ The next time we embark on an initiative, we'll be sure to first consider these options in laying the ground work, such as _____.

✓ When we next face a similar situation (and we will, but in different ways), how should I secure commitments and resources first, before moving ahead, _____.

Reflect on your responses to these questions. The underlying habit or weakness you displayed in each situation that got repeated continuously, resulted from that blind spot. Ask what you can do better next time to tackle those tricky situations and people's reactions more effectively. Keep an open mind while evaluating your reactions.

5. WHAT IS YOUR GREATEST STRENGTH? (IT MIGHT ALSO BE YOUR BIGGEST LIABILITY.)

Every leader possesses natural strengths and capabilities. For some leaders, it means pursuing a project with immediate urgency and focus, in meeting timelines and budgets. For others, their definitive decision-making capabilities carry the day in plugging away with positive results to show at the end of the day (or project completion). Yet others have an emotional understanding of their employees' positions and feelings; and how to factor in team members' abilities to impact the team's overall project successes.

Another way to combat potential blind spots is to consider what liabilities and weaknesses may develop, because of your greatest strength. For instance, one of my clients exudes a lot of confidence in his approach (strength) as he brings people on board for projects. Team members become excited about his confidence in moving forward with decisive decisions. However, this confidence might not make room for contingencies—thus leaving the team unprepared to consider and react to possible contingencies and failures of their new initiative. How will you allow and empower your team members to become more effective contributors?

It is hard for the ego to self-evaluate one's own blind spots. However, making progress means making headway in becoming more self-aware, which is a lifelong ongoing process. When we're more self-aware, it makes it easier for us to align our teams to move forward successfully every time—from empowering ourselves and others.

LIZ'S LEADERSHIP TIPS FOR AVOIDING DENIAL

- To truly empower someone, you need to let go of your fear of losing what you have built.

- Take a deeper dive into the inner politics of your company culture; discover what is ailing that department to better inform your decisions, while saving those who are politically challenged.

- Be the leader who knows exactly how entry-level employees are treated daily; keep your ears to the ground—and make sure everyone knows it.

Chapter 6

• • •

RECOGNIZING DEAD ENDS AND GETTING BACK ON TRACK

Policies are many, principles are few;
policies will change, principles never do.

—*JOHN MAXWELL*

What drives us all to succeed at what we do? The simple answer is—we seek purposeful meaning in all we do, along with the ability to deliver effective results. Are your leaders communicating their unique vision for team members to achieve outstanding results? Do they make team members feel that they are valued and effective? Nobody wants to move forward with a future that has no joy and a career that has no advancement. Our brains release new energy whenever we anticipate future success and growth we can go after, in achieving amazing results. In other words, we're energized when we clearly see a purpose for taking valid action and anticipate something brighter ahead.

FUTURE SIGNIFICANT LEADERS: MANEUVERING WITHOUT FEAR

As a rising star climbing the corporate ladder, it pays to take stock of other people's capabilities, and of your colleagues who are similarly striving. Know that immense efforts are taken by corporate big wigs to figure out who has what it takes to get to the top, develop others, and to reap the glories of leadership potential. You must know this is sometimes a silent observation—even as you wisely climb with personal grace and professional adroitness.

There will be others alongside who are also very determined to lead and reach the top. Therefore, do not be the person who views competitors as "people I have to work apart from." At the same time, "don't give all your secrets away" to other strivers. This is a delicate balance in every corporate or company dynamic. The key to succeeding is, to be very careful about how you manage your confidence and how you affect others along the way, while displaying effective teamwork. It may seem complicated to keep track of these nuances all at once, but it is a necessary strategic approach to become a recognized leader—as you appear to those holding positional titles and behind-the-scenes influential persuaders who possess the unseen power to anoint company leaders.

You need to focus on many things during your climb; you need to continuously keep checking in and honing on your strategic approach. This is key to your development—*reflection*. Are you representing yourself in ways that pave the way for your ongoing successes? Often, I use to pretend that I was on a stage and think to myself about what I would say if many more people were watching me at this particular moment. Today, I find myself on an actual stage often so I pretend I am on international television.

As you reflect on your behavior and the way you present yourself, ask yourself these very important questions: What types of people surround you? Are you perhaps clueless about who may be derailing your leadership aspirations? I am a big fan of constructive employee development and in order to succeed, you must find yourself in an environment that is open to advancing your growth, expanding your mind-set, and providing you with opportunities to learn every step of the way. Or, it may be that you nearing a dead end.

RECOGNIZING DEAD ENDS

This chapter aims to help you reflect on situations and leaders you encounter while climbing the ladder of success—and how to get back on track after recognizing a possible dead end. I will say this: things can sometimes appear as dead ends but are not; you must truly be in tune with your company dynamics and culture, be politically aware, and understand the motivations of those who lead you. In my career, I often have clients who see something as a "dead end" that is actually once we give it a little bit more time and truly understood what the situation's drivers and motivations were. You'll be shocked to learn that many companies have leaders in charge of departments who don't have the time or the mandates to develop their staff or give them opportunities to learn and advance. I have also seen companies where top-tier leaders empower politically manipulative executives to dominate their departments and inflict their self-serving personal agendas to generate results and outcomes benefitting them personally— and often not the company as a whole. These types of leaders usually don't last or win in the end, as I believe true winners are those who inspire other leaders and leave a trail of leaders behind them. Any environment or culture that isn't driven by that authentic desire to empower and advance those that want to learn is not a very healthy one.

This is the reason I'm so passionate about sharing my tips below to prevent you (or help you recover) from being derailed by dead ends. I have met leaders who are unaware how their actions influence some employees; they often don't have time to consider the empowerment of others or the advancement of those on their teams. This doesn't make them bad people; usually they wake up on their own after a major incident, or deep self-reflection that often leads to a wake-up call followed by transformation. I have seen this category of leaders go on to become some of the best I have ever encountered.

I have seen this happen to clients and members of their teams. These leaders can become some of the most generous and self-aware people in the organization. For certain unhealthy behavior to survive, it usually needs to be enabled and supported; otherwise, it gets weeded out of the organization. The tolerance for unhealthy or imbalanced behavior could either be directly coming down from the top, or the company culture may be supportive of it.

I've seen amazingly talented people get fired because of power trips generated by empowered leaders who were insecure deep down. In my unwavering need to help people become more self-aware, I have been able to help a few such individuals understand their actions and how they can affect others. These leaders often cause the company to lose good and talented employees and they also end up leading those who have lost all confidence in themselves and their futures. Worse, it discourages all employees who watch this from other departments from giving their best to the company and its leaders. Terri Kabachnik's book *They Quit and Forgot to Tell You* (2006) discusses this very concept; where employees who are discouraged stop doing everything they can to contribute to the company—while staying put, just to get their paychecks.

Of course, lower-level staff in departments led by people who are perhaps not confident enough themselves and do not empower others as a result, feel completely powerless because they see that this is blindly supported by top-tier company leaders, perhaps silently. Good employees naturally lose all motivation to succeed working in such a demoralizing environment. Those who stay feel powerless to make progress toward changing their department culture; many end up conforming and treating this as "the norm."

Negative repercussions keep growing, and skilled employees who are confident, honest, intelligent, and forward-thinking lose out. So does the company, on every frontier; perhaps not in the short term—but in the long run, when patterns get noticed and turnover increases or continues at the same rate. From a short-term perspective, these types of unhealthy leaders may seem like a blessing; they give those in power exactly what they need to hear and it works very well for a while. Even as the smoke gets murkier behind the scenes, until someone eventually asks, "What's burning?" "Why aren't we putting out fires?"

In such environments, as soon as honest and dedicated employees refuse to support those who don't empower, develop, or help others progress, they usually get dismissed themselves, which may be a blessing in disguise.

Talented, motivated, and determined individuals deserve to flourish in supported and trusting environments, to have real chances for professional development and leadership opportunities. If you provide this for your employees, they usually reward you will their accomplishments and loyalty and inspire teams to produce effective results. You must understand that these opportunities should be authentic, given to employees by leaders who truly want them to succeed. Lean in on leadership opportunities presented by people who truly want to develop and support your professional and personal growth, in alignment with your ethical standards.

CLIMBING WITH INTEGRITY

Some rising stars can sometimes lose sight of upholding integrity and ethics on their way up (refer to chapter 2 where I discuss keeping your soul clean on the way up). These rising stars can become ruthless for a short time, some due to peer pressure and in trying to prove themselves, while other poor conduct was just waiting to be exposed. I call this behavior another eventual dead end. Most who got into trouble because of their dishonest behavior now regret their actions. Staying true to who you are will help you stay out of downward-spiraling situations. Become more self-aware; self-awareness takes you farther and beyond immediate gains.

In addition, it is disheartening to know of ruthless leaders who also brought down their superstar team members with them. The reputations of these rising stars will never be the same again, because often, their progress becomes tarnished and stunted. When rising stars start out on their journeys, they are vulnerable and impressionable; if they ended up working for the wrong kinds of bosses who influenced them to use their talents in negative ways, their careers will mistakenly veer in unintended directions with resulting consequences.

It really pays for rising stars and current company leaders to be cannily aware of, and be strategic in their approaches, to spot and tactically maneuver around unhealthy situations, behavior, and cultures. Similar to a prison, once prisoners riot and gain control, it is too late to rein them. As the saying goes, an ounce of prevention is worth pounds of cure later.

UNHEALTHY BEHAVIOR LEADING TO DEAD ENDS

Any of these tips need to be part of a combination of various behaviors to suggest an unhealthy pattern. The difficulty often is that many healthy leaders are seen as exhibiting a few of these qualities from time to time, due to circumstances surrounding them. It is important to distinguish between healthy and unhealthy behaviors even when they seem similar. A lot has to do with circumstances; there are times when someone may seem to be exhibiting some of these behaviors when he or she isn't or perhaps is forced to. There are also times when leaders are faced with very limited choices coming from the top, and are required to engage in behaviors that are not very healthy for the organization or its culture at that time. This doesn't make them bad leaders or bad bosses; trust your gut when reflecting on a leader's true internal nature.

1. INFLUENCING OUTSIDE OF EFFECTIVE AND ETHICAL INFLUENCING STRATEGIES

As in lobbying, or politicking, in continuously patting themselves or their team in front of higher management. These bosses see themselves as doing no wrong. They're usually first to report on operations within the organization, whether bad or good, to top management. Of course, the good news is almost always coming from their department. Just as the phrase "those who lobby" suggests, they spend inordinate amounts of time ensuring perceptions never match what is really happening behind closed doors.

The caveat for rising stars is aligning behind a leader who gives the impression that everyone on his or her team is great. If that leader is ever questioned, your credentials will be in question. Just as a mirror reflects what you see, an honest boss reflects back your authentic qualities and contributions; and vice versa for unscrupulous bosses and rising stars who are afraid to oppose their "snaky" bosses.

2. NOT HIRING EXCEPTIONAL, SMART, COMPETENT PEOPLE

These executives are deep down fearful of someone seeing through the smoke they generate—that they don't bring to the table as much as they want people to think. They're hesitant to hire intelligent employees because smart people will almost always see through things while working under them. It is much easier to fool colleagues and higher-level executives who stay out of their daily operations.

In some cases, these particularly talented and motivated employees may shine through and upstage them. Worse, intelligent employees will almost always quickly realize they do not want to, and cannot be, led by this type of boss. As a result, the team suffers as a whole, due to the insecurities of its leader.

3. ONLY VOICING OPINIONS AND EXHIBITING REASON IN FRONT OF TOP-TIER LEADERS (C-LEVEL AND BOARD MEMBERS)

They may not say a positive word to their teams, dislike their colleagues, and never encourage their teams or appreciate them. Yet, when they get up in front of an important audience, they very quickly act the opposite way. They enact a performance whereby "our teams are the best," and certainly very lucky to have them for colleagues who teach them every day. They are "lucky to be surrounded by such talent." They are "grateful for the chance to work with such dedicated individuals" in their departments. I call these leaders "the performers." I have watched my clients call this behavior out, especially those clients who operate within an open-door policy with the rest of their staff. If you are working under a person who does this, it may be tough for you to penetrate through to the top. The question becomes "does he or she truly appreciate your talents?"

4. EMPLOYING OUTSIDE VENDORS TO PUSH THROUGH SPECIFIC AGENDAS

Don't get me wrong; I fully endorse bringing on third parties to help inside the organization. I am one of these third parties whom clients employ for just that reason. But, the desire must be agenda-free. The only agenda that should bring consultants to the organization is one where the main focus is a well-defined objective or project. Some leaders get outside professionals to validate their own opinions and to support only their ideas (while not serving the company's needs). These persons love outside firms coming in—but only on their own recommendations.

They want the accolades, and they want to have their own out-side people pushing their agendas from the inside.

The person who is hired usually operates to serve this indi-vidual as a result of getting such jobs through him or her. On occasion, I get invited to participate in projects where other con-sultants are also involved. It has become easy for me to tell who operates without bias, and who is there to push an agenda. This may be a dead end since the leader's objective is often serving his or her own agenda than developing or promoting talent.

5. EASILY DISPOSING OF OTHERS

Especially on those who have ceased to serve their agenda. These types of bosses also often never acknowledge the help or support they received from those whom they have discarded.

6. NOT ACKNOWLEDGING THAT AN UNHEALTHY CULTURE EXISTS

They wave off questions about team leaders manipulating employ-ees, and of looking into a possibly unhealthy culture within the organization. They're usually the first to discourage this analy-sis—the reason often is, they don't want to get their hands dirty trying to get to the bottom of the issue, or they are part of the problem to begin with. It is often a lot easier to deny that it exists and since this approach is not glaringly obvious, it is easy to deflect or deny its existence altogether.

7. MANIPULATING COLLEAGUES TO SERVE PERSONAL AGENDAS

You need to analyze how "partnerships" flow between executives. Figure out if these relationships are mutually healthy, or led by one dominant person who manipulates the other less suspecting person under the guise of "collaborating and supporting one another." Sometimes these collaborations are authentic and supportive. However, be also aware that unwavering support for a leader of another department brings up a different set of questions, such as, why is the support so unconditional? What is the real motivation behind this kind of support for one another? Sometimes it can be due to a real friendship and support; other times, the reason could be more sinister.

8. USING VENDOR RELATIONSHIPS FOR PERSONAL GAIN

Some leaders have special vendor relationships. This is very common and can be very honest and healthy. Some leaders, however, use company resources and their purchasing power to hire vendors for their own ultimate gains, even when they are personal in nature. I had a client whose director used his power to hire vendors in a bartering system that ran for years unnoticed. He hired vendors at exaggerated prices that cost the company unnecessary money, picking in return what he wanted for personal use.

Graft and bribery are silent operators you need to be aware of. If you work for this type of boss, he or she will eventually be exposed; with the department questioned as a whole. Your reputation is then at stake especially if you are in a position that was perceived as close to the boss. It is very important to note that you must investigate this type of claim thoroughly. Often, what seems like a personal relationship may actually be very ethical and professional; watch and evaluate very carefully before you make this determination.

9. NEGATIVELY DIVIDING AND CONQUERING TEAM MEMBERS

I am not completely against this method when applied in a positive and healthy way to keep everyone honest, but many people who use this method, misuse it, thereby creating severe mistrust. These bosses will usually have "a flavor of the month." Meaning, favoring the person who does their grunt work; in turn, these "team players" consider themselves to be inside the loop and "good friends with the boss."

Such behavior results in other team members feeling less committed in being part of a unified team. This kind of boss drives wedges between team members to make it easier to win over anyone by instilling fear. Obviously, a united and friendly team stands stronger against one built upon lies, deceit, and continuous questioning of trust.

10. LEADING EMOTIONALLY DISTRESSED STAFF FEARFUL TO SPEAK UP

Team members do not speak up because they're fearful of losing their jobs, because this executive leads with fear and unspoken intimidation. Many distressed employees will speak if pressed; allow them opportunities to share their concerns. The overall department attitude appears to be "emotionally off," with people silently putting their noses to the grindstone.

Invariably, some team members will veer toward exemplifying the unhealthy leadership style their leader displays. They feel comfortable telling lies, in wanting to get ahead. In getting away with presenting work others have helped them generate and sometimes "massaging" information to get the results they want.

SOME TIPS TO KEEP THINGS HEALTHY

✓ When someone seems "off" check out his or her HR files and recheck all references (of course, with proper authorization).

✓ Personally call referees yourself to check on the executive leader you hired; don't leave this task to HR.

✓ Take junior people to impromptu lunches; you'll understand better how their boss functions on a daily basis; then draw your own conclusions about how these wide-ranging opinions may affect the team.

✓ Meet with people who don't work for the company and give them the opportunity to speak to your group; later, get reflections from those individuals to find out who may be in distress, or what department needs help.

BRINGING BACK HARMONY AND PRODUCTIVITY

You could conceivably be the new leader hired to replace an unhealthy leader who bled the company of talent because of his or her greedy, underhanded tactics. What would you do to heal a shocked, confused team?

TAKE CARE OF YOUR PEOPLE

The most important first step is to take care of people on your team. Show you genuinely care, and *want to work together* in healing a shocked department. They are people who have been there for your company, perhaps with decades of seniority under their belts. People who were left out in the cold when your department was shattered. They were left demoralized in not knowing what happened, what to do next. If needed (because you were an in-house candidate ultimately selected to be the new boss), take responsibility however intangible your role was, by admitting your lack of self-awareness in being unaware of the situation that festered so disproportionately.

To start healing an unhealthy environment and to maintain your leadership edge, take these steps:

- ✓ Reassure them that moving forward, you'll work together as a harmonious team where everyone gets a fair share and is respected for his or her efforts.
- ✓ Everyone's opinions and feedback will be seriously considered.
- ✓ Lift up their spirits and inspire them to give their all again—under the best of circumstances (with you at the helm).
- ✓ Tell them their jobs are safe.
- ✓ Tell them they are appreciated for their work and contributions in every way.
- ✓ Tell them they'll have opportunities beyond what's going on today.

Although it took a very long time, a client of mine took a significant step in terminating an executive who was very troublesome and who participated in activities to hinder not only his team but also the entire company. The CEO admitted having missed many red flags. He brought me on to assist with department morale after the termination. There were over twenty individuals in the department—directors, managers, lower-level staff. The termination came as a complete shock to everyone on the team.

However, once we dug in we found most of the staff had been feeling very oppressed. They were shut out of the entire operation with the exception of two people working alongside that department head. It was a challenge to figure out how to get these individuals back to an emotionally secure place where they'd feel confident about their employment, contributions to the company, and be no longer fearful; to welcome sharing their feelings with honesty and transparency.

Long ago, I came up with a role-play activity I called *Occupy the Chair*. I have shared this with a few clients prior to bringing it to this company and had great feedback. We rolled out this program whereby every week at their company-wide management meeting, one person from this department came in to talk about how he or she honestly felt. The person were to also share what they felt was lacking in their terminated boss, what qualities they'd like to see in their next boss, what the areas of neglect were, and whether or not they were lacking necessary resources to perform their jobs successfully.

We reassured everyone that the goal was to help get this department back on track. We made sure they knew we were not just looking at them as vessels of information post termination (a very common feeling when bosses get terminated where the common expression is, "They called me in to find out what was going on"). Every company needs to combat this unfounded impression first, before moving on.

The first few persons found it difficult to speak because they were uncertain about what had happened to their terminated boss. So, we turned the approach around and told them the story before they had an opportunity to share anything with us. We were very transparent. *(Some people still want to fight the fact that things are changing, and companies are becoming a lot more transparent where employees are empowered.)*

We explained why this termination occurred and how we envisioned the department to work in the future. It was amazing to watch my client, the CEO of this organization speak from his heart, displaying immense admiration and care for his employees. I'm honored to have been included in these meetings to witness these emotionally intense interactions. We made sure they understood that troublesome terminations were part of business operations needing to be worked through. We made sure they understood that *solutions post higher-level terminations were important* for the morale and survival of their department. We assured them we were 100 percent dedicated to a successful turnaround and asked for their help. As we shared what happened, we bonded with employees every week. Each week, we came closer to understanding how they felt trapped inside a department under a boss who didn't let their talents and highlights shine through.

My client was astonished to find how talented some employees were and to find that he had absolutely no idea pure gold was hidden away by this terminated executive. Some lower-level staff communicated with us as if they held executive positions. Their communication efforts were very effective. They were calm and patient as they reflected on their years of service under this troubled boss. Some were extremely well-educated; for some, their passions were writing and graphic design, while others wanted to work for other departments in the company. We finally found out they'd communicated their desires to switch to different departments years ago, but were never considered.

Occupy the Chair served us well during this period because it was mutually beneficial. My client promoted the administrative assistant supporting this group's sales and marketing projects to Manager of Sales Analytics for the entire company. He raised her pay significantly, as well. This woman was very proficient with software programs; she did the job of a data analyst for years, never saying a word. We were astonished and dumbfounded listening to her data analytics and software-reporting capabilities.

It took months to see everyone in that department. However, after the first five, our communication style spread like wildfire. People became excited to talk to the leadership team. The presence of other executives and department heads proved to be worthwhile, with talented employees from the affected department ending up working for them. While getting to know these employees, we told them that part of the reason was to help them choose their future boss. I agreed to assist my clients in this search but only after we gave everyone the chance to speak his or her truth. This exercise single-handedly won loyalty and dedication. Employees regained their enthusiasm from participating in choosing their new department head. Some department heads expressed to my client after the exercise that they wanted something similar for their departments, too (even though no termination was involved) because they really wanted to get to know their staff this way.

TRANSPARENCY LEADS TO TRUST

Many young leaders I coach voice their number-one issue as: the feeling that top management teams keep major initiatives from them. Many do not even get simple feedback on reports and projects their teams have completed. The only way to truly boost morale and ensure the *health of the organization throughout* is to *apply preventative measures throughout the year.* To me, ensuring transparency with staff is one of those measures. You can tremendously diminish backlash with this strategic approach.

LIZ'S LEADERSHIP TIPS FOR STAYING ON TRACK

- Learn to spot the boss who will never let your light shine; that person holds the dimmer.
- Ensure you are communicating company strategies directly to your employees; don't leave them in the dark on important decisions.
- Work toward a healthy culture and call out behaviors that display a resistance to responsibility, accountability, and transparency.
- A boss who empowers you must also enable you and provide continuous support to ensure you aren't being set up to fail.

Chapter 7

● ● ●

RISING TO THE TOP AND MAINTAINING YOUR EDGE AS AN EFFECTIVE LEADER

There are three qualities a leader must exemplify to build trust: competence, connection, and character.

—JOHN MAXWELL

Everyone sees the world differently. However, there is one sterling, singular law that is immutable: no matter what your position is, to be committed to honest principles. Instead of changing policies that were put into place by other people whose ideas may not work for you now that you're at the helm of a company, team, or project—stick to your principles as a leader whom other people will come to trust, respect, and enjoy working with and for.

Adopting this simple strategy will ensure you conduct your leadership style in ways that irrefutably and continuously honor what you truly believe in, and live by, as an outstanding role model. Show the world your impeccable leadership standards, in reflecting how hard you worked to reach the top, and are continuing with sharpening and maintaining your leadership edge. And, that you are just as determined to continue working as an inspiring leader who knows how to wield power effectively, while garnering respect and trust from people who love working with you.

DEVELOPING LEADERSHIP

I often get this question from millennial clients I coach: "How do I gain trust from my colleagues?" There is no simple answer. As I've been iterating all along, your team members will learn to trust you when you support them with integrity and show competence in working hard along with them. Here are four tips for developing your leadership style and efficacy.

POLISH YOUR COMPETENCY AND CHARACTER

John Maxwell is a leadership visionary who stresses the importance of allowing your *competence and character to build trust* with those whom you lead, or will eventually lead. You must allow your true competence and character to evolve over time—from watching authentic leaders and learning from mistakes (which are, after all, pillars to success). How you adopt and adapt leadership lessons from watching authentic leaders will be your lifeline as a powerful leader.

There really is no substitute for learning from our experiences (positive, negative, and everything in between). This is very important. Reflect on what you have learned and how to be more prepared to meet contingencies the next time around. In addition, I observe from my own and client experiences this astounding insight—that unless we identify root causes of what, where, and how we made mistakes, this underlying root cause will keep on rearing its ugly head in many other subtle ways. Hence, it pays to spend time reflecting on what triggered your initial glitches—and how to overcome obstacles.

For example, as I explained in the previous chapter, unless a company CEO learns to become more self-aware and aware of his company culture and his team or departmental leaders, bad bosses who are manipulative leaders will continue operating silently, ultimately destroying or deflating the company over the long haul. This is how I've found that nipping problems in the bud early on with an ounce of prevention is worth pounds of efforts to detoxify departmental operations later on, to regain staff morale, and to ultimately rebuild the company's brand identity and productivity.

DEVELOP *YOUR* OWN UNIQUE LEADERSHIP STYLE

What does it take to develop your own unique leadership style? Natural leaders may be born leaders. However, even born leaders need to learn from observing how authentic leaders conduct themselves professionally. Such as in negotiating and closing deals, keeping their ears to the ground to know how their department heads operate and treat team members, even taking phone calls with professional courtesy and business-like manners. Seriously consider these ten coaching tips I continuously reinforce with clients to enhance their brand identity as respected and trusted leaders, and continue as top-ranked leaders in their fields. These tips will help you develop your own unique approaches to understand what truly works and stands out in all aspects of leading and creating worthwhile projects for your team's competitive edge.

TEN TIPS FOR CREATING YOUR UNIQUE, LIKABLE LEADERSHIP BRAND

1. Turn people *on*. Your colleagues and team members should want to be around your energy (maybe they can't figure out why they're attracted to you). You inspire them no end by looking at and solving issues in refreshing new ways.

2. Be *emotionally seductive* in a professional setting with your leadership demeanor. People must see you're not a

robot. They have to be able to envision when you make it to a leadership role that you'll have a level of maturity, sensitivity, and emotional connection—that you're not robotic and mechanical with your responses. On the other hand, do not be too emotional, either; keep that balance in check.

3. Don't be a pioneer of opinions; don't connect yourself too closely to controversial causes, especially in our intensely politically driven world. Believe that people are emotional, and can very quickly end friendships and careers over strong opinions. Keep yours to yourself. Respect that people have varying opinions on virtually every issue, particularly controversial and sensitive ones. It took me a while to learn this particular one; passionate people are usually passionate in all aspects of their lives.

4. Ask for assistance and create an opportunity for others (especially those more senior) to help you. Additionally, you can never stop saying thank you when they do.

5. Stay away from creating or being a part of any drama, negativity, or awkward moments with senior members. Stay respectful even when you do not agree with their decisions. You haven't been privy to the larger scenario they're operating in, with valid reasons for taking temporary steps in the interim.

6. *Never dread* being exposed to senior staff members and leaders through projects and communicating your ideas (however, do think them carefully over, first). If you have nerves, you *cannot* let those around you know that exposure makes you uncomfortable. Take the opportunity for high-level exposure and opportunities that come your way. Run with them, and impress everyone!

7. Don't expose your weaknesses; don't speak about your successful parents or family connections; don't explain how you achieved amazing results for projects (don't gloat); and don't bring up too often past issues and problems with authority figures.

8. Come from a place of *yes*. Then think about how you will accomplish working through whatever you agreed to. Always say *yes!* to the right people (leaders you care to align with). Recall my story about the thirty-four-year-old who was offered a VP position? Even though he did not have the chops there and then, he reflected upon the opportunity and very creatively acquired the competencies required for his new job.

9. A little less extreme excitability, a little less complaining and in using the word "can't," a little less urgency.

10. Results speak loudly! Stay focused and balanced as a thoughtful, reflective leader as you climb your way up. No clawing or bragging rights are needed. Just focus on delivering actionable results.

BE WILLING TO DEFER IMMEDIATE GRATIFICATION

Mastering the ability to defer or sacrifice immediate pleasure and personal gratification while working hard on opportunities is a challenging lesson for most ambitious people to learn. Many can't grasp the need to do the hard, grunt work first. Then, when an opportunity presents itself, you need to jump at it and be ready to give up pleasure and free time for that unique opportunity. You need to cancel whatever previous leisure or pleasure plans in order to work hard, to take advantage of that unique opportunity showing up unexpectedly. This is an important principle to stress. Whenever I speak to college students getting ready to join the workforce (with many shouldering the burden of immediately repaying student loans), I emphasize this point.

It is important to persevere in the face of daunting odds. Ask every successful leader—and he or she will tell you it wasn't all roses and peaches getting to the top. Many have had to endure numerous stumbles, falls, rejections, and failures. The important lesson here is to get up, learn from our failures, and never ever give up pursuing our goals. John Maxwell's advice is pure gold:

> **Don't ever be impressed with goal setting; be impressed with goal getting. Reaching new goals and moving to a higher level of performance always requires change, and change feels awkward. But take comfort in the knowledge that if a change doesn't feel uncomfortable, then it's probably not really a change.**

CONTINUE DIGGING INTO YOUR SELF-AWARENESS

Anyone who is truly self-aware can accomplish anything. Whether you're dealing with climbing that ladder to success or looking down on your teams, you have to be aware of who you are and who you are not. How do you lead? What are your weaknesses? Are you constantly aware of circumstances that impact the decisions you make? I want you to truly dig deep inside and see what it is that's stopping you from propelling forward. Most times, you'll discover it's because you're not certain of who you are, yet. People who know themselves well are not tainted nor affected by the opinions of others or their put downs. Instead, they could probably relate every negative experience to a time when they learned something more about who they truly are. The lesson here is to turn around every negative experience into a positive one.

Self-aware leaders continue to rise and conquer every obstacle because they know exactly what their talents and weaknesses are, while moving forward. This type of confidence is not cockiness shouted out from the rooftops, but a quiet self-reliance, self-assurance, and resilience that enables you to understand your pitfalls as you lead others. The more you discover yourself and accept who you are, the closer you are to leading with confidence and instilling trust in your followers and team members.

MAINTAINING YOUR EDGE AS AN EFFECTIVE, POWERFUL LEADER

Once you've reached the pinnacle as a respected leader, your work begins. Most people are too focused on climbing the ladder, and unaware that they must work even harder to maintain their position upon arriving there. The higher you go, the tougher it becomes to maintain your position. When you have expended all your energies trying to be recognized, you must also understand what it is that you are trying to reach for as a leader. Stay hungry even as you reach the heights you have aimed for, stay motivated, and continue to strive for excellence.

TIPS FOR MAINTAINING YOUR STRENGTH AND POWER EDGE AS A SUCCESSFUL LEADER

1. Make sure you have what it takes. Hopefully, if you have made it into a leadership position, you have mastered this one. Motivation and ambition without competency, required skill sets, and the talent to perform is a waste of time. Again, the key here is self-awareness. I pointed out before, "You must know your weaknesses." You need self-awareness to climb high, and embrace what's waiting there.

2. Risk it! You won't get far without making risk a leadership attribute. Quietly challenge the norms and procedures of how things get done in your workplace. Keep innovating new and efficient ways of doing specific tasks. Do *not* announce that operations are inefficient and you'll be taking on the challenge to hit reset. Nobody likes a new leader on a power trip. You need to risk taking on the initiative of being efficient and effective; keep presenting well-thought-out ideas to people above you respectfully and then help your team deliver as a leader who gets his or her hands dirty along with his or her team in presenting deliverable results.

3. Volunteer for tough tasks that are seemingly undoable. Upon completing them, the more senior leaders or board

will look up to you as someone who can take on difficult, challenging, and uncertain assignments and lead his or her team through successfully. Such a person quickly becomes the "go-to" for the entire management team.

4. Avoid suicide missions; never embark on a failing task, in order to impress. All this accomplishes is shining a negative spotlight on your efforts. Not all publicity is good publicity. In reality, it is quite the opposite; you write every detail of your reputation as you go along.

5. Do not be one-dimensional. To keep on maintaining your leadership edge, senior leaders must not pigeonhole you as "one-sided, structured, and not flexible." One-dimensional thinkers almost never make it to significant leadership roles. Leading large numbers of people with flexibility is a must to achieve results for the entire team.

6. Exhibit true devotion. You need to continue to be committed and devoted to your work in authentic ways. Upon reaching a leadership role at any level, this becomes even more important. Your devotion needs to be real and genuine. The key here is, for everyone to remember you had dedication in working your way to the top and you kept your dedication once you got there. Assure senior leaders that devotion will play out in your new leadership role, as well.

7. Contribute in a different way. Take on employee-engagement challenges and create ways your team can collaborate to be collegial and united. This makes you stand out because this is how quality leaders prove their worth—in uniting strong teams achieving results. Show it! Present ideas for team motivation and engagement. If these ideas are good, other department heads will absorb them and have your name on these innovative ideas; perhaps even the CEO will hear about it.

8. Control! Control! Control! I speak about this a lot. Control your words and actions around your team and senior leaders. Every action and expression should have some Bubble Wrap around it. This is your career and your future; you just have to be cautious. Corporate environments are all about 90 percent people watching your moves and listening to your words. You are watched and judged—at every moment. Control what you put out!

9. Create relationships with the *right people* in the organization (there are always people on the inside privy to all sorts of info; reflect on chapter 3 explaining Political Savviness). Prepare ahead of others by being privy to information and position yourself and your team in front of the right person(s) especially if your desire is to climb even higher, or there is someone on your team deserving

of an opportunity to be awarded them. When you stay close to the right people, you continue on at a different level compared to other people in the organization. Knowledge is power.

10. Make sure you truly want your leadership status. Some people just love their comfort zones and don't know it. Be cautious when climbing; you might get your wish, and regret ever having aspired to be a high-level leader. At this stage, you will be tested as to whether or not it's a good idea to keep climbing. This is true in leadership development as it is for college; many drop out in the first year.

ALWAYS AIM FOR TEAM COLLABORATIONS

Company-wide collaborations can only be achieved when employees believe their leaders are self-aware, and not led by a few unscrupulous team leaders who are there for their own personal gains and agendas. Healthy interdepartmental collaborations happen when management teams consist of people aiming for successful company-wide outcomes. Collaboration between departments and managers is achieved when every employee feels he or she is treated fairly. The more transparent the leader is, the more respect you earn, because this results in your team members wanting you, their leader, to succeed with their support. When they truly root for you, you have achieved their undying respect, support, and collaboration.

Maintaining a healthy transparency is key because it percolates down to the rest of the organization. A leader's desire to collaborate for the sake of the greater good is infectious; be the cheerleader for group work and united award-winning team efforts.

As I've been emphasizing throughout this book, there are two very significant leadership themes current leaders and rising stars need to consider. First, become increasingly more self-aware—not only your own strengths and weaknesses—but as important, of those around you be they positional leaders or influential persuaders who wield unique leadership powers. Second, always uphold your integrity and your line of morality that you draw for yourself in being very selective about the leaders you align with.

Why? Your reputation primarily depends on these two very significant factors I've been discussing as major themes for this book. Self-awareness and alignment are integral and essential in making personal progress and for professional successes.

ONCE YOU MAKE IT, CLEAR THE SMOKE
PENETRATE YOUR TEAMS

Take time to understand the political dynamics of your organization; unnoticed dynamics are generally responsible for increasing turnover. Don't just rely on your department execs to deliver what's going on within the organization. Often, it's too late to save talented and motivated employees buried within the political culture. Don't just occasionally dive in; dive in often.

CHALLENGE AND TEST DEPARTMENT HEADS

Many C-level execs feel they can hand over complete power and decision-making authority to their executives, but it isn't always smart—especially if you don't know them well. Allowing those you hired to do their job properly is key; I do not suggest micro-managing them. Rather, periodically take an unexpected dive into what they're doing to see how they're managing so they understand you're watching and are involved in what they're doing. A good idea is to develop a casual working relationship with two or three team members to ensure the department head is acting with integrity and treating team members fairly.

STOP TOLERATING LOW-PERFORMING STAFF

Executives often make the mistake of tolerating low-performing staff. Winning companies and leaders do *not* tolerate low-performing staff. You can tolerate mistakes; mistakes are different and handled differently. Red flags signaling low performance include a toxic attitude and lack of accountability that negatively affect the workplace. Usually, by the time this person is terminated tremendous damage has been inflicted—damage that takes time to reverse. Such employees penetrate the depths of company culture and are very tough to call out. The time it takes for the CEO to become aware of this imbalance depends on how good the low-performing employee is at manipulating, hiding, and projecting his or her intentions.

DON'T MEDDLE MID-PROJECT

Some executives feel they need to inject themselves into work carried out by their teams. They like to meddle mid-project when things still need resolving, and often assume their staff is losing track. Some of my clients who are department heads often identify this troublesome issue. Do not meddle mid-assignment! Project leaders work hard to tear everything apart so they can piece everything back to deliver great results for the company.

Injecting yourself and acting as "the solution" frustrates team members. Your team would be immensely discouraged if you just popped in and assumed things were mishandled. If the boss showed that he or she didn't trust employees, employees will not give their full efforts either—resulting in downward spirals thereon.

Stay vigilant in becoming more self-aware and aware of your timing in following up on projects and with people. Remember the role of alignment in putting together team projects and team members. The next and final chapter lists my top fifteen leadership lessons gleaned from successful influencers—great insights I continue to use in coaching clients today.

LIZ'S LEADERSHIP TIPS FOR CLEARING THE SMOKE

- It is a tough battle to get to the top; once there, the battle to maintain your edge begins.
- Strive to achieve inspirational leadership, not positional leadership.
- Don't keep cold hard truths from others, and most important, from yourself.

Chapter 8

● ● ●

TOP FIFTEEN LEADERSHIP LESSONS FROM SUCCESSFUL LEADERS

The mediocre teacher tells. The good teacher explains. The superior teacher demonstrates. The great teacher inspires.

—WILLIAM ARTHUR WARD

Learning from observing others is priceless. I learned from watching, listening, spending time with, and being mentored by, influencers who were masters of their leadership destinies. Here are the top *fifteen* leadership lessons I learned.

May the art of observation (and innovative adaptation) guide your own self-discoveries for ongoing leadership insights and ideas.

1. LEAD WITH KINDNESS

In watching leaders deliver feedback to their teams, I saw the most successful feedback came from an authentic kindness within. This compassionate attitude was very evident as the leader spoke to staff. I could see the leader was very interested to enhance and help staff members progress to higher levels of success and performance deliveries on the job. Interestingly, they are also kind to themselves, in understanding that they can make errors—as shown by encouraging their teams to shoot holes in approaches they had suggested.

Lesson: You can't achieve great coaching, leading, and meaningful feedback without kindness.

2. MAINTAIN HONESTY AND INTEGRITY

Honesty and integrity are integral to the organization's health and security. Lead with integrity—it shows. I've watched leaders who had ample opportunities to turn onto darker, more subversive roads; however, they consciously chose to stay off negative pathways. Top leadership needs to encourage honesty and integrity by first being honest themselves. Leaders need to accept oversight feedback and errors in judgment from their managers and supervisors, and funnel this approach down to others below. This attitude encourages self-awareness (something I keep reiterating in this book as a major key to success); where team members learn to understand themselves and their choices better, in watching you make one honest decision after another.

Lesson: Everything starts with who you are, deep inside. Be a leader who walks the path of integrity, self-awareness, openness, and honesty—and you'll be rewarded by attracting like-minded employees to your team.

3. FIGURE THREE TO FOUR STEPS AHEAD: SHORT-TERM THINKERS LOSE

I learned this when I was younger and began to understand what that meant when I started my first business. Today, I may be doing it a little too much as learning this leadership tactic has made me much faster in anticipating contingencies. I have learned to slow down, to become more effective with my clients. An effective strategy requires several moves ahead and contemplating all possible outcomes resulting from those moves.

I use the stoplight analogy with clients (that I'd learned from a successful leader). Leaders need to see a few stoplights and cars ahead of them, in order to quickly assess road conditions, plan to reroute, slow down, brake, and perhaps duck onto a side street. Thinking short term is a strategy destined to fail, both in leadership and at home.

Lesson: You cannot expect to plan your reaction successfully if you can't see past tomorrow.

4. LEARN TO TOLERATE DISCOMFORT AND WORK AROUND IT

I learned quickly to get comfortable in fussy, uncomfortable, and potentially damaging situations. I learned that in order to succeed in my work, to be open to new ideas, and to dedicate myself to serving people and their needs, I'd better learn to feel comfortable with the uncomfortable. The leader who taught me to get cozy with this feeling did so by example.

This leader always seemed to invite challenges. If his day was too comfortable, he wasn't happy. He needed issues to tackle and resolve, opportunities to define more properly, and someone to become better at his or her game, at all times. This isn't necessarily the best way either; there needs to be a balance to the way you lead. However, he taught me this important lesson as I watched him waiting impatiently for meetings and encounters that others dreaded.

Lesson: Get comfortable in uncomfortable situations. This is only a perceived and momentary pause; stay open to fully experiencing unpleasant and uncomfortable emotions.

5. KNOW YOUR CORE TEAM MEMBERS' STRENGTHS AND WEAKNESSES

One leader taught me how vital it is in continuously building upon the strength of the company from knowing what teams are capable of, with the good, the bad, and the ugly. I watched him make quick judgments related to his leaders. He knew very quickly if stories from lower-level staff were true, based on knowing who his team members truly were; and what they could or could not have done.

Lesson: You know what's going on when you understand the capabilities of those involved.

6. AGE IS NOT INDICATIVE OF WISDOM

Stay open to opinions of those who may not have as much experience. New blood brings its advantages. Previous experiences are wonderful for lessons in hindsight but it also taints us with previous rejections, and disasters may make us unnecessarily overly cautious in avoiding potentially winning deals. Listen to what new, young, and not very experienced dynamic persons have to say—fight the natural inclination to tune in to the experienced while tuning out newbies.

Lesson: Talented and intelligent people who at a young age went on to do incredibly successful things were newbies at some table, at least once before—and learned fast.

7. YOU CAN'T PICK AND CHOOSE WHAT YOU WANT TO ACKNOWLEDGE AND WHAT YOU WANT TO IGNORE

Many leaders avoid dealing with complicated or uncomfortable issues. It somehow makes them feel that acknowledging unsavory issues makes them a worse or weaker leader. *But,* it doesn't work this way. Choosing to only deal with (or deal with as priority) issues of a positive nature and ignoring problems or putting them off to another day is counter-productive for every business.

One company leader I know is desperate to come into her office each morning to deal with what she calls "the dirt" first— to get it out of the way for the rest of her day to be more pleasant. Her assistant separates all of her appointments and documents to review into "morning" and "afternoon" categories; morning is for "sifting through the dirt."

Lesson: Get it all out in front of you, no matter how dirty; deal with it, before you're forced to deal with something huge—that had been smaller.

8. WATCH OUT: A STRONG POLITICAL OPPOSITION MAY BE DEVELOPING BEHIND YOUR BACK

There are many examples of the toughest and most talented CEOs failing, because of their inability to manage relationships, and preventing a strong opposing environment from forming. And in the process, driving away great employees. Many people fail due to this phenomenon of not being politically savvy. Not only CEOs. I've seen staff at all levels fail at this need to be more aware; many don't even see it's there and affecting them every day.

Lesson: Tune In to your company culture; be very curious, ask questions, and call out the unacceptable behavior.

9. ALWAYS FOCUS ON CUSTOMER RELATIONSHIPS

One of my earliest experiences watching a large sales team operate is how this particular C-level leader treated the customer. He watched the customer from the moment a deal was struck and made sure to check up on the health of the deal repeatedly thereon. He never forgot the customer, even though he had thousands of them. He once told me, "Do you know what a responsibility you take on when they say yes to you?" I reflect on this often as I coach my clients. I take on a great deal of responsibilities from the minute I agree to help. This is a lesson I will likely never forget; your customer is everything, don't forget him or her. We get so wrapped up in policies, procedures, employee issues, and various other tasks that we sometimes forget the most important part of the business, the customer.

Lesson: Upon getting your customer, tenant, or client, you can't shove it into a drawer; in fact, this is when the real work and relationship development begins.

10. DO NOT SUGARCOAT TO WIN TRUST

One leader was very adamant to not sugarcoat challenging issues in front of his staff. He told me that when you sugarcoat or gloss over situations, employees can see what the real issues are. When they are aware that you're hiding visible issues, it makes them trust you less. I watched as he revealed details to his team that other leaders wouldn't have done, in an honest manner. Over the years, I have seen how much trust and respect he has garnered from his staff—due to his being transparent and honest. He wasn't revealing every single detail to the staff, but enough big-picture directions were transparent to gain trust and ensure that staff isn't functioning in a culture filled with doubt and uncertainty.

Lesson: Making things sound a lot better than they are will soon have your staff lose trust and faith in your leadership.

11. BRING ORDER TO CHAOS

The boss cannot create or participate in generating chaos. Instead, the leader has to break up chaos and steer the team back to harmonious working relationships. However, many leaders don't know this is a very necessary and challenging responsibility they must undertake. The leader should return rational behavior to the team by showing team members ways how the situation will work out; plus ensuring the team adopts a fearless attitude throughout a difficult transition time.

One of the best ways to encourage rational thinking is by taking accountability for the current state of affairs and its eventual correction. By taking accountability, leaders encourage their teams to operate under responsible leadership through a challenging period, which boosts trust and loyalty. When a company's new or changed processes and initiatives get going, the best leaders bring a level of order in strategically organizing and-rolling out new tactics.

Lesson: Chaos or order starts with the leader and the way in which he or she manages and communicates every initiative or action to his or her teams—make it positive and orderly.

12. ENCOURAGE COMMUNITY AND SERVICE

One leader I worked with had three major charitable causes she involved her team in every year. They discuss these incredibly important community causes in ways they would discuss ideas generating profit for the company. This leader puts resources (staff) behind these community causes and ensures everyone understands how important it is, to participate and give back to communities. Bottom line: it's good for business and in retaining employees.

Lesson: When employees know that the company as a whole cares for people, you retain more staff and promote a sense of dedicated selfless giving and service.

13. LEAVE STAFF IN CHARGE OF MAKING DECISIONS

A miraculous thing happens when you hire competent people, and leave on trips without too much preplanning with them. One of my clients does this frequently. He leaves at crucial times, and his core team makes unforeseen decisions surrounding very important projects. My client also takes his time when responding to e-mails from his core team leaders (especially when the e-mail asks for his input with regard to pending decisions). He tells me that by the time he responds, he hopes these team leaders have given it very serious thought to go ahead with decisions they made.

He is aware that they may make different decisions than he would, but he spends a lot of time developing and speaking with his staff with the goal that they retain those values and thought-processes when he isn't around. This is a great step toward contingency planning, as well. The main requisite is to hire very bright, resourceful people to begin with.

Lesson: Enable your team to make the right calls by being unavailable sometimes. This strategy empowers individual team-leadership building, builds team-leader confidence, and allows these leaders to bring the same trust to lead their dedicated teams.

14. TO LEAD EFFECTIVELY, BELIEVE IN PEOPLE

I learned from a leader early on that encouraging people to perform better necessitates making them feel their self-worth and to show you appreciate their contributions. When you believe in people, you help them work on their own self-esteem. They invariably ponder, "If a person at this high-level success trusts me enough to do it, then why don't I trust myself?"

I watched a client who trusted and believed in her staff (even when there were moments I wouldn't have done the same). This didn't guarantee her success every time; yet when given to the right persons, it did wonders for their progress, their loyalty to the company, their confidence-building, and their abilities to make improved decisions moving forward. I experienced this personally when such a leader believed in me; soon, I started believing in me, too.

Lesson: Show people you believe in them; make them feel important and worthwhile of your time, your appreciation, and your confidence in them—which ultimately pays huge dividends.

15. ADDRESS ISSUES IMMEDIATELY, IN PRIVATE

The man who taught me this runs a highly successful company, surrounded by extremely competent employees. He always was, and continues to be adamant, about resolving matters in private—rather than in front of other team members. He's very passionate that people don't get away with an action or communication that could hurt the company or other employees, or a decision that he felt was plain wrong. The result is, he gets heard ASAP by the person he feels whom he needs to confront. He does this very quickly, not waiting for time to elapse after the issue arose. He finds it important to deal with issues while passions are running high and to resolve them immediately.

The only thing he is more passionate about is *doing it in private.* He has always been very sensitive about how team members are perceived by other team leaders. He ensures every leader can keep his or her head held high in front of others. However, deep down, he understands he or she needs to be called out at various times to resolve issues amicably and quickly.

He does not do this in a negative way though, and uses it as an educational opportunity for ongoing professional staff and leadership development. I continue to alert my clients to ensure that all confrontations and issues to be resolved be carried out in private, and very soon after the incident or decision. As the saying goes, there is a place for everything, and everything in its place.

Lesson: Do not break a person's self-esteem and his or her confidence around other team members by confronting or calling him or her out publicly.

It is my honor and pleasure to be able to share this book with everyone who is working towards self-awareness, alignment, understands the importance of mutual benefit and aims to uphold integrity through smoke-filled situations. This book was written with intense passion that I hope you felt on every page. Continue working hard, stay true to yourself and your principles and your future will continue to shine bright as you get closer and closer to your ultimate dreams.

LIZ'S FIFTEEN "SMOKE AND MIRRORS" LESSONS

- Strive to achieve inspirational leadership, not positional leadership. This can be done from any seat.

- You cannot inspire another, if you aren't inspired yourself.

- Quiet your mind, and listen to your intuition.

- Find a fair balance between being assertive and collaborative.

- No one cares about the reason you cannot do something. People are focused on getting results—get busy delivering results.

- Respect your haters, they will help you succeed; then turn around and help them succeed.

- Know your weaknesses, write them down, and reflect on them daily. Don't participate in or initiate projects that mostly require skills you have identified as your weaknesses.

- It is a tough battle to get to the top; once at the top, the battle to maintain your power position begins.

- Burn bridges only when someone has imposed upon your morality or ethics.

- Don't focus on crumbs; look for the loaf of bread. Strive to win big battles, not trivial ones.

- Simplify everything placed in front of you; nothing is really that complicated. Others want to make it appear complicated to make their contributions seem greater; don't let them.

- Leading someone to do his or her job well is much harder than doing it yourself.

- Be the leader who knows how entry-level employees are treated daily; keep your ears to the ground, and make sure everyone knows it.

- A spotlight only benefits if it's impressive—not destructive.

- If you're not obsessed with your goal, get out of the way, and let someone else achieve it.

READING LIST

Adams, Scott. *The Dilbert Principle: A Cubicle's-Eye View of Bosses, Meetings, Management Fads & Other Workplace Afflictions.* New York: HarperBusiness, 1997.

Babiak, Paul, and Robert D. Hare. *Snakes in Suits: When Psychopaths Go to Work.* New York: HarperCollins, 2007.

Bailey, Sebastian, and Octavius Black. *Mind Gym: Achieve More by Thinking Differently.* New York: HarperCollins, 2014.

DeLuca, Joel. *Political Savvy: Systematic Approaches to Leadership behind the Scenes.* Berwyn, PA: Evergreen Business Group, 2002.

Dixit, Avinash, and Barry J. Nalebuff. *Thinking Strategically: The Competitive Edge in Business, Politics, and Everyday Life.* New York: W.W. Norton & Company, 1993.

Ferrazzi, Keith, and Tahl Raz. *Never Eat Alone: And Other Secrets to Success, One Relationship at a Time.* New York: Crown Business, 2014.

Gimbel, Tom. "How to Tell if a Potential Hire Has Emotional Intelligence." *WSJ*. March 12, 2017. https://blogs.wsj.com/experts/2017/03/12/how-to-tell-if-a-potential-hire-has-emotional-intelligence/

Goldstein, Noah J., Steve J. Martin, and Robert B. Cialdini. *Yes: 50 Scientifically Proven Ways to Be Persuasive*. New York: Free Press, 2010.

Hewitt, Sylvia. *Forget a Mentor, Get a Sponsor*. Cambridge, MA: Harvard Business Review Press, 2013.

Howard, Ronald A., Clinton D. Korver, and Bill Birchard. *Ethics for the Real World: Creating a Personal Code to Guide Decisions in Work and Life*. Cambridge, MA: Harvard Business Review Press, 2008.

Kabachnick, Terri. *I Quit But Forgot to Tell You*. Largo, FL: The Kabachnick Group, 2006.

Maxwell, John. *The 21 Irrefutable Laws of Leadership*. Nashville, TN: Thomas Nelson, 2007.

Pfeffer, Jeffrey. *Managing With Power: Politics and Influence in Organizations*. Cambridge, MA: Harvard Business Review Press, 1993.

Phipps, Mike, and Colin Gautrey. *21 Dirty Tricks at Work: How to Beat the Game of Office Politics*. Oxford: Capstone, 2005.

Simon, George K. *In Sheep's Clothing: Understanding and Dealing with Manipulative People*. Marion, MI: Parkhurst Brothers Publishers, 2010.

Vaynerchuck, Gary. *#AskGaryVee: One Entrepreneur's Take on Leadership, Social Media, and Self-Awareness*. New York: HarperBusiness, 2016.

Witz, Greg. *Lead, Follow, or Get Out of the Way: The Ultimate Guide to Leadership in the New World of Business*. Toronto: CreateSpace, 2014.

ABOUT THE AUTHOR

Elizabeth Dulberger is an executive coach, adviser, and speaker. With her passion and extensive industry knowledge, she founded the Dulberger Group to educate, train, and motivate current and future leaders through coaching, seminars and workshops. Her unique and intuitive approach  to business and personal successes continue to inspire clients in various industries and countries. Elizabeth's background includes transformational leadership, business management, workplace conflict resolution and negotiation, mediation, and facilitation.

Elizabeth has worked with companies in various industries, including small and large Fortune 500 companies, successful start-up entrepreneurs and politicians. She speaks at industry conferences, company meetings, and corporate retreats, plus colleges and business schools to prepare those entering the workforce.

Advancing People and Organizations
e.dulberger@dulbergergroup.com
www.dulbergergroup.com

73806328R00104

Made in the USA
Columbia, SC
22 July 2017